(continued on next page)

ALSO BY LAURA SHAINE CUNNINGHAM

A Place in the Country

NOVELS
Third Parties
Sweet Nothings

PLAYS
Beautiful Bodies
Bang
*I Love You, Two (Where She Went, What She Did
and The Man at the Door)*
Cruisin' Close to Crazy

SLEEPING ARRANGEMENTS

Laura Shaine Cunningham

RIVERHEAD BOOKS, NEW YORK

Riverhead Books
Published by The Berkley Publishing Group
A division of Penguin Putnam Inc.
375 Hudson Street
New York, New York 10014

A portion of this book was originally published in *The New Yorker.* Portions of this book were based on *Hers* columns by Laura Cunningham, which were originally published in *The New York Times. CPP/Belwin, Inc.*: Excerpt from "Hi-Lili, Hi Lo" by Bronislau Kaper and Helen Deutsch. Copyright 1952 (Renewed 1980) by Metro-Goldwyn-Mayer, Inc. Rights throughout the world controlled by Robbins Music Corp. Assigned to EMI Catalogue Partnership. All rights administered by EMI Robbins Catalog, Inc. International copyright secured. All rights reserved. Used by permission. *Polygram International Publishing, Inc.; Warner/Chappell Music, Inc.; Peter Maurice Music Co. Ltd.;* and *Redwood Music Ltd.:* Excerpt from "Isle of Capri" by Jimmy Kennedy and Will Grosz. Copyright 1934 by T. B. Harms Company, Chappell & Co., and Peter Maurice Co. Ltd. Copyright renewed and assigned to Chappell & Co. and PolyGram International Publishing, Inc. Rights in Canada administered by PolyGram International Publishing, Inc., and Redwood Music Ltd. Rights in the open market administered by Peter Maurice Music Co. Ltd., London WC2H 0EA, and Redwood Music Ltd., 14 New Burlington Street, London W1X 2LR. International copyright secured. All rights reserved. Used by permission.

First Alfred A. Knopf hardcover edition published in 1989
First Plume trade paperback edition: January 1991
First Riverhead trade paperback edition: July 2000
Riverhead trade paperback ISBN: 1-57322-823-0

The Penguin Putnam Inc. World Wide Web site address is
http://www.penguinputnam.com

The Library of Congress has catalogued the Plume trade paperback edition as follows:

Cunningham, Laura.
Sleeping arrangements / Laura Cunningham.
p.   cm.
ISBN: 0-452-26557-6
I. Title.
[PS3553.U478S5   1991]
818'.5403—dc20   90-14274
[B]   CIP

Printed in the United States of America

10 9 8 7 6 5 4 3

To my uncles
And in memory of my mother

I wish to thank Victoria Wilson,
Daniel Menaker, Owen Laster, and Daniel Strone
for their help and enthusiasm.

I began my life waiting for him. When other children asked, "Where's your father?" I had my mother's answer: "He's fighting in the war."

For the first four years of my childhood, I grew into the anticipation: my father would come home when the war ended. Until that time, my mother and I moved in a holding pattern from one relative's apartment to another. Sleeping on sofas and collapsible cots, we squeezed into odd slices of space. I awakened looking up at the undersides of a dining table, with my mother wedged beside me between chair legs. In the dark of different living rooms, we traded questions and answers that were always the same:

"Did he see me before he left?"

"Once. You were in your crib sleeping."

"Why didn't you wake me?"

"You were fast asleep."

How could I sleep through my single chance to see him? Something's amiss. From the shadow of the dining table I demanded more details.

"What did you wear to the wedding?"

"A beige suit."

"Not a white wedding dress?"

"There wasn't time. He had to fly overseas."

His legend grew, as legends do, in his absence, on the strength of repetition. He could fly a plane, fire a machine gun. He won more medals than anyone. And—this was my favorite detail—he had his own fighting dog, a boxer named Butch, who was a gentle pet when he wasn't ripping apart the enemy.

Who was the enemy? My mother was vague as to the exact identity of the opposition, but specific in attending to our patriotic duties. On national holidays, we hung a dime-store flag from the window. At parades, we sang on the sidelines. It was a red-white-and-blue story, told to the accompaniment of bugles. There was only one flaw: while we waited for my hero father to return from battle, this country was not at war.

No war. I heard the news and rushed to tell my mother, who, in 1950, assured me that World War II was still underway. "Most of the soldiers have come home," she conceded, "but there are still a few outposts that have to be captured."

While my father fought at his faraway front, my mother and I lived in limbo. The interrogations continued—I collected information:

His name was Larry. He was from Alabama. His hair was blond, his eyes were blue. My mother stressed superlatives: he was the handsomest man she'd ever seen; the best dancer. His hair was "so blond it looked white in the sun."

Pressed for evidence, my mother produced a snapshot of Larry, which she showed to me only when we were alone, only at night. This photograph was as transient as we were—my mother rotated its hiding place. As often happens with an irreplaceable item, we concentrated so hard on its safekeeping that it was often misplaced, usually disappearing between the pages of books. We wept when the picture was missing, but never considered having a duplicate made—the risk of entrusting "him" to a photo-processing store was too high. As soon as I could write, I penciled on the reverse side:

The only picture of my father. Big Reward.

Not only was this snapshot elusive, it was overexposed. Technically black-and-white, the photograph, taken in an Army office, seemed to have acquired the khaki color scheme of its setting. My mother and Larry appear in shades of beige, divided by a cone of light so bright it threatened to disintegrate them. By the mysterious method of film, this snapshot seized its own truth: the dissolving dazzle of the soldier at its center. So radiant was he, he might have been the light that blanched the negative.

Beside his brilliance my mother appears blurred—a dark woman whose expression can't be caught by the camera. Her blurriness is profound, as if, at that time, she was so unsure of herself that she could not be clearly photographed. There are such times, when the camera can only record confusion or evasion, the mind turned inward. In person, my mother had a physical habit of ducking sudden, unpleasant truths. Did the camera catch this characteristic dip of her head? Whatever the cause, she is forever out of focus.

My father sits at his desk. Surely, it's his desk. A cigarette burns in the glass ashtray beside his hand. He looks up, a dent of irritation between his pale eyebrows. Interrupted at work?

My mother stands beside him, and because of her blurriness, she projects an impression of movement, of having just stepped into frame. She is flanked by a second woman and another officer, a pair of "strangers" whom my mother and I would have loved to scissor out of the photograph.

The strangers didn't belong in the picture. My mother and I never said so, but we felt that the unknown couple spoiled what we could otherwise regard as an informal wedding portrait.

There was a great deal of precedent for excising unwanted figures from family photos. Our album exhibited a heavily revisionist approach. On almost every page cousins had been cropped from group portraits. Sometimes the entire bodies had been removed, but more often only the offending heads, which gave our family photograph collection an odd, mutilated look. Here and there, couples could be seen in an embrace, but one had been beheaded, leaving a mate with his arms around a well-dressed torso. More women than men had been scissored out of the record, suggesting that the cut-and-pasteup of family history had been executed by a third party. Eventually, I came to know the woman responsible: my grandmother. Years later, I caught her in the act, bent over a group picnic scene with scissors and a razor blade.

Her photo-editing sessions were the closest she ever came to domestic endeavor.

My mother and I had none of her malevolent zest. Instead, we collaborated on an alibi for the unknown couple and incorporated them in the scenario: No longer "strangers," they could be "witnesses" at the wedding.

Whenever we stared at the snapshot, my mother recited her tale of rushed romance: the lunch-hour wedding, a goodbye kiss on the tarmac. As she spoke, I envisioned my mother and Larry dashing from the khaki world of the war office into an exterior that was also overexposed. I saw my mother and father race across the bleached streets of noontime Miami Beach, toward a whiteout of a wedding.

Soon, I noticed that my mother colored when anyone asked questions about Larry. Her voice rose high—she almost could not aspirate; "husband" became a gasp for breath. I, too, felt a squeeze on my windpipe when my father was mentioned. It was hard to lie, even if I didn't know the truth.

The fabric of my mother's cover story frayed fast. We were stranded in an awkward interval between wars. My stories of a father "fighting overseas" incited serious interrogation. Other children, teachers, neighbors wanted to know "Where?" Soon, I became the prisoner of war: I didn't want to answer anymore. Sometimes I said, "The Pacific"; other times I whispered, "Europe," which I pictured as a continent-sized Oriental carpet laid out across the sea.

At last: Korea. What a relief. My mother and I could relax on the home front. At least no one looked at us askance and asked, "What war?" anymore.

But even the Korean action came to an end, and with it the first installment of life without father. One afternoon as I demonstrated mock machine-gun fire—"This is how my father kills them"—my mother tapped me on the shoulder and led me a discreet distance from the other girls. As we talked, she said I shouldn't tell that story anymore. I guessed the reason.

"The war's over?"

"In a way it is." Larry would not be flying home after all. His body was already buried overseas. I asked about the medals, the ribbons, perhaps his uniform?

With a vividness of detail I can appreciate in retrospect, my mother explained why there was nothing left to be sent to us. "He was blown up in tiny pieces." His uniform burned, his medals melted, the ribbons charred and lost forever.

Butch? Was Butch riding in the tank? No, he was not. He was on guard duty that day. "The Army needs dogs like Butch." Butch had been reassigned. And so, it appeared, were my mother and I.

No longer transient, we moved to our own efficiency apartment. We were no longer ladies-in-waiting; we were in mourning. On the first night in our new home, my mother lit a memorial candle, and set it in the corner of the bathtub, there to flicker in remembrance without becoming a fire hazard for twenty-four hours to mark my father's death.

$\mathcal{O}$ur move had the effect of a magic trick. We changed households in minutes. Our belongings were as portable as we were: everything we owned folded. We moved by subway; my mother with a cot under one arm and a card table under the other.

We left behind our previous accommodation in the narrow living room of an elderly aunt, a crevasse of an apartment set in a medieval-style building itself constricted between two look-alikes. This Gothic housing complex, modeled emotionally as well as architecturally upon feudal times, managed to capture the hopelessness of the era that inspired it. Designed around a sunless courtyard with a defunct fountain, this development appeared inhabited by a nation of Old World munchkins, whose growth was distorted, like bonsai trees, by the ropes and bundles attached to them. A horsedrawn cart seemed to rattle over from Europe, driven by a man of medieval appearance (no teeth, grizzled beard), who cried out in a caw that was unintelligible but had something to do with "old clothes."

My mother and I fled these shadowed parts for what she called the "wide-open spaces." Wide-open they were. Our train tore from the subway tunnel, as if escaping the dark past, and skidded to a halt at our stop, the first outdoor station on the line.

We stood at the edge of the Bronx, on a crest that overlooked the river and Manhattan. Between us and Manhattan lay an infamous whirlpool, which was known to have sucked boats and barges into its spiraling depths, then spit them up as splinters.

There was no mistaking the whooshing uptide in my

mother's spirits. She sang as we walked through the dark streets to our new home. Our past had been a string of sequential Sundays, looking, always looking for a place of our own. We'd toured so many model apartments that our dream wafted this specific scent: new pine and shellac.

We arrived at our first apartment: a fresh white studio, with an el, its floor still tacky with resin. We entered on tiptoe, walked the borders, careful to inhabit the place gradually—or it might disappear. My mother lit the memorial candle, and so, serviceable as well as sentimental, this beacon to Larry's memory illuminated our new home. My mother cast a magnified shadow on the walls.

With only a single cot, my mother and I had to initiate new sleeping arrangements. I couldn't quite believe that we were alone, that we could choose where we would sleep. (Although, never having known a bed or a bedroom, I didn't mind sleeping under tables. There was a coziness to claustrophobia, even an accidental elegance; when the tablecloth was left on, my mother and I luxuriated in the canopied effect.) All I ever needed to drift off, feeling snug, was to see her familiar silhouette—the curlicues of her hair, the deep curve of her hip. She was the single constant in my changing nights, my campsite mate in the carved forest.

While I'd always been near her, I had never slept touching her. Now, for the first time, we tried to share. Together we moved the single cot against the wall, for the sense of fortification. I climbed onto the sway-backed military cot (a last link to Larry, who was said to have lugged his Army bed from Europe to Korea).

My mother slid in beside me. It was summer, and her skin scorched. We lay there, our minds ticking, aware almost audibly of each other's thoughts. I inched toward the abyss of the empty studio, my effort to create distance as palpable as a complaint. Tense as a troubled marriage bed, our cot sagged under the double weight and the realization: this arrangement could not last the night.

My mother volunteered to lie on the floor. She stretched out on top of her dress. Stricken—had I hurt her feelings?—I reached down and touched her hand.

In the morning we showered together. By day, our studio was bright, somehow Scandinavian, divided into geometric patterns of light. And in this bare room, empty as modern art, our romance began.

As happy as newlyweds—alone at last—my mother and I danced with fruit in our hands and celebrated the morning. We were free to be together in ways that had been impossible with screaming cousins and irritated aunts yelling in the cramped corridors. Wearing towel turbans and terry-cloth sarongs, we exulted in our new privacy: ecstasy in 3M.

3M, I saw by hard daylight, was set into a building of schizoid design. While the exterior was blandly modern white brick, the interior was decorated in a style that might be called Babylonian Bronx. In the lobby, murals depicted scenes of Dionysian excess, and mosaic maidens walked a deluded diagonal along the walls toward the mailboxes. The mood and the maidens came to a dead halt at the elevator door. From there, it was a short ride from Babylonia-in-the-Bronx to seven stories of "worker" housing cubicles that could easily fit into Stalingrad. The housewives of AnaMor Towers pushed their wire grocery carts across marble lobby floors, rode the "Ionic" elevator up to "junior fours."

9

The dual nature of AnaMor Towers (named for the owners, Anna and Morris Snezak) was conducive to the secret life I would lead here: outwardly ordinary, inwardly ornate, owing all inspiration to heathen cultures. I suspected the other tenants felt a tug, too. Who could be immune to the libidinous lobby? I soon discovered the other little girls in AnaMor Towers were deeply indebted to pagan ritual for routine play. How could we avoid it? Every AnaMorite had to pass a frieze of Pompeii on the way to the incinerator.

AnaMor Towers did not stand alone. The entire neighborhood was a cross section of ersatz bygone cultures. In the park, marble mermaids lounged, with rust running down their navels. Public buildings were supported by semi-nude figures, wearing New Deal chitons. Many of the apartment buildings were modern Towers of Babel, mixing details from Ancient Rome, Syria, Greece. (In retrospect, one wonders if the Jews who designed these edifices were paying some delayed tribute to ancient enemies.)

On my way to kindergarten, I saw that the neighborhood became increasingly extraordinary. There was something inhuman in the scale of the streets. The avenues seemed overly wide, suitable only for mass invasion. The main thoroughfare, Grand Concourse, was a reproduction of the Champs Élysées, with the substitution of Yankee Stadium for the Arc de Triomphe.

The old stadium dominated the area in more than a merely physical way. Built for ritual on a major scale, the arena cast a spiritual net that extended at least ten blocks. (My mother and I soon discovered that AnaMor Towers, a few streets from the stadium, stood on a baseball fault zone. The building reverberated with collective roars of victory or groans of defeat. Twi-night doubleheaders cast an insomniac glow into our efficiency, and night after night my mother and I would lie sleepless, bathed in violet light, listening to megaphoned moans of "It's a homer! It's a homer!"

Golden, softly rounded, the old stadium had a Biblical look. I assumed it had been standing on 161st Street since before Christ. (Years later, when I saw the actual Roman Coliseum, I couldn't suppress an inner gasp of recognition: "Ahhh, it's like Yankee Stadium.")

My mother and I passed the stadium on our way to our separate destinations: she went to work, and I to nursery school. We breakfasted at a diner intended for baseball fans. Even off-season, hot dogs rotated on racks of anticipation. We were ravenous as lovers after a long night.

We had to say goodbye at the nursery schoolyard. She kissed me through the Cyclone fence. The other girls lined up too, as their mothers filed past. The children competed: Whose mother was the prettiest? Cries of "Mine" echoed down the line. We ran along the fence to the last possible point of contact, then pursed our lips through the chain-link for "a last one." The mothers planted their kisses, then ran for the subway that took them to "jobs" in the great unknown of "downtown."

Uptown, caged into our reservation, the secret day began. Divided into age groups: threes, fours, and fives, we played at tribal rites, primitive as aborigines. The leader girls forced their followers into scatological ceremonies—to "make" in a carton, kept beyond the teachers' sightlines.

Elaborate scenarios were enacted. I assumed a second self,

Deer Girl, a Sioux Indian maiden. As Deer Girl, I led hunting parties across the asphalt. There were enemy tribes afoot—even the
noble Sioux were on the warpath.

During my first week in the nursery school, I staged an escape: With two other fives behind me, I scaled the fence, only to
be recaptured by a guard. When my mother was told I led the in-
surrection, she said, "Lily always had leadership traits."

She gave me a costume, a Deer Girl dress: fringed and embroidered with the symbols of the rising sun and a crescent moon.
In full regalia, I played Indians for hours at a stretch. There was
nothing innocent in the game. (Why do adults talk about the "innocence of childhood"? All I remember is the intuitive guilt.)
Without official knowledge of sex or death, we flirted with both.
When we found a dying rat in the play yard, I saw a ribbon of ex-
crement unfurling from its rear end, and announced that all living
things left the world that way. (It may be true but how could I
know?)

The boys were warriors, loved enemies, to be feared if no
teacher was looking. It was understood that an unguarded moment was an opportunity for assault. We girls knew that if we en-
countered a boy in a secluded place he would either hit or kiss us,
or perhaps want to watch us "make." In turn we tantalized them:
swinging upside-down on the monkey bars, knowing our panties
were "showing."

In all our Indian games, the girls fled from capture. I didn't
understand the details of what would happen post-capture, but I
knew enough to keep running. To be carried off would fulfill my
wildest fears. I must fight, scratch, kick, then perhaps give in to a
frenzy that could not even be imagined.

We all feared being stripped. Threes and fours were stripped on a regular basis by more powerful, savvy fives. In the playground, the enemy was omnipresent, ready to pounce, tug down your panties, and "see."

As one of the faster girls in the nursery, I escaped being "seen," but protecting my "privates" was an almost full-time job. The school sanctioned more nudity than I would have allowed. The coed toilet—the BOYS commode beside the GIRLS—offended my sensibilities, and I conspired not to join the urinary lineups. Couldn't they put up a partition? In a similar spirit, in hot weather, we were expected to "change" into swimsuits "in front" of each other. Squirming on the linoleum floor, I wriggled off to a discreet corner, faced away from the crowd. I peed in a secret "club" carton (only a few select fives were allowed to use it) behind the schoolyard's lone bush, took to wearing my bathing suit "underneath."

Curiously, I was also modest at home. I asked my mother if I could wear my underpants in the bathtub. "Of course," she replied.

At kindergarten, I suffered a single, serious setback. One winter afternoon, I couldn't pull my pants back up, and had to hobble, bound by underwear at the ankle, into the public room. I was immediately taunted—as I knew I would be: "Look, she's wearing two pair." (Well, it was cold.)

I went to kindergarten as if into daily battle. There was only one respite: nap time, when we stretched out in rows of cots, like Civil War wounded.

After school, I often returned alone to the apartment, dense in its atmosphere of solitude. On many an afternoon I spent this time gazing into a terrarium on the windowsill. In this miniature glade, a china figurine—a girl—appeared to be pursued by a youth with a bow and arrow. I invented scenarios, with alternating plots. Sometimes she was fleeing the boy; at other times she was leading him to a secret forest. As this situation evolved, I rubbed the tiny vitreous china figures. Stories seemed to require gesture. As the chase accelerated, so did the massage. After a time, I wore the paint from their porcelain tunics, exposed the coarse white bas-relief. In a similar fashion, I often held a doll, and, without awareness of my actions, worked her plastic eyelids up and down. I owned a dozen "dollar" dolls, whose eyelids and limbs I dislocated: Cinderella developed a permanent astigmatism, and Snow White's arms were twisted round in their plastic sockets. I was hard on their costumes, too. During my agitated imaginings, I rubbed off the nap, leaving them threadbare across the breasts.

Apart from these small gestures, I sat quite still at the windowsill, waiting for my mother to return from work. I peered into the terrarium "forest" or stared, unseeing, out onto the street. If darkness descended and my mother had not yet appeared, I became more alert. My heart hammered alarms, until I would see her at last—her wraparound coat flying open, as she ran down the street.

Sometimes, she caught me unawares, glassy-eyed in the twilight of the windowsill. I might gasp and blink: iridescent bubbles dotted the air. These bubbles were linked, like atoms, and it took a moment to clear the air and re-enter the spirit of our studio.

These temporary departures were my lone journeys to another place. Apart from the joy of being with my mother, these secret soarings were my most pleasant moments. A buzz in the blood, a reprieve from the dull tick-tock of real time—transports of delight.

I could not tell time. The symbols on the clock at school puzzled me. At home, the moving wands on our Emerson clock radio had a reverse effect: mesmerized, I lost more time than I found—hours could pass while I watched. But I did have some sense that the hands were intended to keep track. I knew the design for "three"—that was when school let out—and the straight line of "six" meant my mother should be home soon.

When not hypnotized in a sun-soaked stupor, I ran free in the neighborhood. Sometimes, I roamed alone, but more often I played with either Diana or Susan.

Diana and Susan were the only other girls on the loose in this part of town. All the other little girls were supervised, chaperoned to ballet or piano lessons.

Pleased to be victims of benign neglect ("We're so lucky no one watches us"), Diana, Susan, and I exceeded our mothers' wildest fears. We jumped from rooftop to rooftop, balanced on ledges, and swung from fire escapes. Daily we courted death and sexual disaster.

In those lost afternoons and early evenings, it was sometimes hard to choose between the radiance of daydreams and the equivalent adventure on the street. In each, there were impassioned pursuits, magical escapes. . . .

My mother didn't know the life I led in the interval from three to six. "You're careful, aren't you?" she asked.

And I always answered, innocent on a technicality: "I look both ways."

*D*iana.

At five she is the object of male attention: grown men stare and young boys give chase. For her wildness and her beauty she is sometimes stoned—a situation that she is able to handle: Diana always carries a weapon, a stick or a stone.

Diana is a dirty blonde in every sense. Her forearms show pink streaks, tributaries of cleanliness charted by accidental contact with water. She seldom bathes, but the dirt doesn't detract from her appearance. Her filthiness functions as a natural cosmetic, and has the effect of a tan, accentuating her blondness. She looks like a miniature starlet—pink pout, waist-long tangles of hair. As she runs across the rubble of the city lots, she appears like the tiny heroine of an after-the-A-bomb nuclear stone age epic. In her torn clothes, she has a soiled sexual appeal. Her eyes, however wide, are not quite innocent.

She has a little tagalong sister, Nan. Nan is also blond, but has only one blue eye. The other eye was put out with a dart, thrown by a baby brother when he was only two. Nan is often with Diana, usually slightly behind and to her left. On command from Diana, Nan will remove her glass eye and offer it for inspection. She can hold it in the palm of her hand, like a hard-boiled egg, or set it into an optometrist's case, rather like a jeweler's box for a brooch. Sometimes, to be comfortable, Nan likes to run around without the glass eye anyway, and the empty socket makes her face pucker, turn prematurely ancient. Her remaining eye appears dilated in fear, as if she anticipates yet another terrible accident of fate.

Diana's exotic, even to me. A French Catholic in a Russian Jewish neighborhood, poor among the lower middle class (or the upper lower class, depending on who's pigeonholing whom). Diana lives in the slum-next-door, a tenement somehow left over by the developers, a sliver of a brownstone that seems to lean against its higher, huskier new neighbor, AnaMor Towers.

She lives on the top floor of a six-floor walkup in four small rooms, packed wall to wall with mattresses and box springs. The rooms are mercilessly sunlit, every abraded board and cracked wall exposed. The paint seems to peel almost energetically— falling to the floor, like latex leaves, in an indoor autumn. Even by day the roaches run—across the floor, up the walls. At night they are a fast-moving guerrilla army, and can turn a wall black at the flick of a light switch. The many members of Diana's family have an almost unconscious habit of roach killing. They slap at them with their shoes, without any comment or interruption of whatever other activity is underway. Sometimes, the Duvals stage raids on the roaches: deliberately allowing a room to remain dark for a few hours only to invade, slippers held high, for a few minutes of roach mass murder. The apartment smells of the roaches and the sprays sporadically used against them.

Their furniture is the sort usually seen left on the street for garbage pickup (which is where Diana's father found it). The sofa appears to have been rained on, its arms sagging, its belly gutted.

Children sleep everywhere, in litters, on mattresses that are squeezed into every room. When I "call for" Diana, I often find her asleep, under Army-surplus blankets—lying diagonally among assorted brothers and sisters: she is one of seven.

Diana's mother, Mrs. Duval, is a heavy blonde in whom despair has taken the form of relaxation. She is as worn and unsprung as the easy chair in which she always sits: a great lump of chintz, parked in the kitchen.

Mrs. Duval has bleached blue eyes, the color of her duster, the same shade as her chair. She seems content to sit through life, sucking diet candies. She allows us to eat any after-school snack we crave. She oversees the preparation of spaghetti sandwiches without editorial comment. While other mothers campaign for fresh foods, Mrs. Duval works a can opener without complaint; even her spaghetti comes from a tin. She sits and watches us eat starch, as her other "kids" try to destroy the furniture, which is beyond damage. A stationary matriarch, she rules from her chair. She sits, and sees, and occasionally produces more children, with the same slack ease that is her style. She never yells. Perhaps she doesn't have the energy, but I think this is also her nature, her sedentary goodwill.

In the Duval apartment, I can never pinpoint a place where Diana's parents sleep. There is no such area as a master bedroom. Diana's father is a professional thief and is away at work all night. At dawn he reappears, dragging duffel bags filled with household goods. Thin as his wife is stout, Mr. Duval doesn't seem to require sleep. All day, he lies wiry and awake on the sagged sofa, a weak radio squawking near his ear. Mrs. Duval, I imagine, must sleep in her chair.

The senior Duvals cannot be caught sleeping, let alone mating, yet they have produced seven children and the end is not in sight. Wildly divergent in age and height, the kids range in age from their mid-twenties to eighteen months; they are all beautiful blue-eyed blondes. They look alike (the same face stamped out in different sizes and sexes) and when at home wear only stretched-out, no-longer-quite-white cotton underpants as a sort of family uniform. Their bodies are always on view. Diana walks around bare-chested with a casualness I would never emulate. All the Duval children are slim, despite their pure starch diet, and have long legs and jutting behinds.

The eldest, Donny, is twenty-two, Cupid-faced with a blond pompadour, who has come home after "serving in Korea." He has come home in earnest—that is, he shows no sign of leaving the apartment. He is a permanent object in the living room and occupies a second sofa, equally unsprung, across from his father's. For years, Donny relaxes into the sofa's declivities, and calls out for more soda and beer, which his sisters serve him. There is something sensuous about Donny, lying there in his jockey shorts, as if he were a preview of the adolescent boys who lie in wait a few years ahead. Languid and indifferent, Donny occasionally throws us nickels. Diana and I dive onto his body, in a monetary *ménage à trois,* coming up with change.

At the start of my association with the Duvals, my mother hired Mrs. Duval to mind me after school. The professional arrangement failed the first day, when Diana led me out of the radius of her mother's chair and onto the rooftops and streets. Outside, we gravitate toward the garbage-scapes of the lots, where we play Indians or construct elaborate forts. We find an abandoned sewer, and call it our "cave."

In poor weather, we retreat to 3M, for the privacy. There, without the watchful eyes of either mother, we slip instantly into that shared state which may also be the essence of sex: a spell in which Diana and I assume other identities.

We play out scenarios that owe something to the seraglio décor down in the lobby. We wrap bedspreads around our hips and undulate through dust columns of light. We walk the diagonal of the maidens in the mural, hold out our hands, and turn a semipermanent profile. I whisper involved tales of our lives in palaces and temples, how we are forced to dance and worship new gods and conquering kings. My mother returns to 3M to find us vanquished, slumped to the waxed floorboards. Sometimes Diana's game takes a violent twist. We must be murdered, she says. We stage the event. My mother unlocks the door to find our two bodies smeared with grape-jelly gore, the butter knives at our sides.

Why do we have to do this? I want to know.

Diana always has the same answer: "Because."

No one has ever known a girl as wild as Diana. At five she is already notorious—it seems as if her reputation has been around longer than she has. "*A shand und an scandal*" is the usual denunciation when she runs past grown-ups. How can she be allowed to run free? (The question should be, Who could stop her?)

The neighbors have many suggestions—that she be spanked, seized, sent to foster care, an institution. Her parents have long since given up even attempting discipline. Diana boasts: "I can do anything I want. . . ." Her monologues often consist of bragging: she stayed up until one in the morning, she drank coffee, she sneaked into the subway. . . . How much is true, and how much is her imagination, I have yet to discover. But she does lead me into one exploit after another. Small even for five-and-a-half, Diana shows me how to duck under the turnstiles at the el station; we ride for a stop. Such journeys for unescorted five-year-olds are unheard of—except for Diana. But then almost everything about Diana is unheard of.

Soon I share her reputation. Mothers of nice girls forbid their daughters to play with us. A hiss of "wild Indians" can be heard as we streak past the other mothers, who are parked in aluminum folding chairs in front of AnaMor Towers.

Diana gives me her unexpurgated guide to the neighbors: The white-haired grandfather in 2J, who looks so nice, and always offers us candy, is not what he appears. According to Diana, he secretly pees on the candies, then rewraps. I now know enough not to ask, "Why?"

The woman in 2K, her hair permanently set in rollers, will throw pots of water from her window on us. She, too, appears on cue, to poke her head out the window and yell, "God will punish you."

(There is a God of AnaMor Towers—a vindictive voyeur who finds no misdemeanor too minor. Make a face and He will freeze it. Disobey your mother and He will make you sorry when she's dead.)

Above all, Diana warns, we must stay out of range of the super. She tosses an unlit cigar in his basement window, then, as we run, explains, "He hates kids."

"How could that be?" I wonder, fleeing. I love "kids," dream of creating a separate little city for us, a junior Oz. Diana and I even pinpoint the location—a demolition site that features a crumbling fountain. From the roof of AnaMor Towers we can look down and see a master plan for the development we call "Kiddietown." The population of Kiddietown will be under ten years old, and the floor plans are inspired by our game of Ropes and Ladders. No disapproving neighbors or supers will be allowed within the walled city.

My mother is the only mother on the block to allow her child to play with Diana. And even my mother makes sporadic attempts to tame her. When Diana's baby teeth rot, leaving her with a great black smile, it is my mother who takes her to the dentist.

Diana cannot be examined. Even the dentist is impressed. She leaps from the dental chair and scales a file cabinet. No one can coax her back to the chair. As the dentist chases her, she runs, like a squirrel, along the walls, finds the door, escapes, cavities unfilled.

My mother takes Diana to the hairdresser. Again Diana escapes, this time with her hair half cut. Her blond bangs remain disparate for years.

Diana will not take off her big sister's communion dress. Her mother, the teachers, everyone has begged. Weeks, months after the event, Diana still wears the white tulle dress, with mesh veil and headdress. The dress is now gray, the hem drags. She is a soiled miniature bride, clutching a cracked plastic purse. I am mad with envy.

"Become a Catholic," Diana proselytizes, "and you get the dress." She leads me to her church and a Catholic academy, set on a knoll overlooking the Grand Concourse. The garden is filled with statues of the Virgin Mary and other saints, whose crucifixes Diana has ripped off, and which she now wears, the chains turning green around her neck.

The Catholic school is called Ursuline Academy; the name is spelled out in giant white plaster letters placed on the grassy hillside. I sit in the U, as instructed, but refuse to convert.

Instead, Diana and I practice our own religion, a form of animism, in which we worship specific bushes, stones, and trees. Our communion in this faith is profound. We have only to exchange a glance, at the sight of a particular tree stump, to "know." Our unanimity at play is prolonged; we spend entire afternoons enacting tribal life.

I come to know Diana's feral ways: She bites without reason. She can turn from playmate to enemy and issue harsh commands: "I want you to walk around outdoors with no top."

Hands on hips, she swaggers in demonstration: "See. I walk with no top."

Her tiny nipples seem to turn inward, for their own protection. "I walk with no top," she repeats, in menace.

I won't. She hits me with a stick. I try to catch her gaze, to reestablish contact with the "other" Diana, but a shade has fallen behind her eyes—the rage. She doesn't see me.

Most of the time, however, she is fun, and it is Diana who shows me the hideouts. Our new neighborhood is extreme enough for her games. This section of the Bronx features stone staircases hacked into the hillsides, where projects stand, like pueblos, at the edge of the abyss. There is a bridge that leads to Manhattan, directly to a museum that features shrunken heads.

Diana and I are the most regular visitors at the Museum of the American Indian (we go there to get ideas). All one of us need say, to start a pell-mell dash across the bridge, is "Want to see the heads?"

The heads are lined up neatly in glass cases. Their lips are sewn together with heavy thread. Some of the heads are the size of tangelos, but the hair remains—long, coarse, savage hair, hanging in a matted tail, not unlike my own.

"Wild Indians." We can't hear that compliment often enough.

*E*very baseball season, Diana and I look forward to the annual visitation of the godlike Yankees, who march across Grand Concourse. The Yankees encamp in the area's only luxury hotel, the Concourse Plaza, which is a sports-oriented Ritz, covered in glitz. Everything that can be gilded has been. I can't imagine a more momentous event than the arrival of the Yankees at the Concourse Plaza. The Yankees—sturdy, handsome—seem to arrive to save us from some fate (as indeed they do—the economy of our neighborhood depends on the season).

Am I the only one who thinks Mickey Mantle may be more than mortal? His alliterative name, his batting average, the very word "Mantle"—all seem to imply he may be more than human. I regard Mickey Mantle as enjoying some in-between status—part human, part deity, all Yankee. (Is this wishful memory or did they really wash the street before he crossed it? I know they set down an actual red carpet. And why not?)

To an extent, I lead a baseball-dominated life. Not only does the stadium emit strange lights and sounds—my mother and I soon become accustomed to the twi-nights, accept them as naturally as Norsemen must have tolerated their endless days in the land of the midnight sun—but the entire neighborhood is designed around the sport. Bronze statuettes of baseball heroes pose at the intersections like signposts. I pass "Babe Ruth" on my way to school, meet Diana at Yogi Berra Plaza. Every day, I walk through an outdoor baseball hall of fame.

In season, the streets are clogged with fans; the entire neighborhood is redolent of frankfurter. Off-season, the area's exaggerated scale becomes a problem. The width of the avenues diminishes the residents, turning their ordinary outings to buy groceries into marathon treks. There's no doubt our area is designed for more dramatic events—a stage set for the multitudes.

It's disquieting to see the empty stadium. It too soon takes on the look of a ruin, evoking those ancient arenas of Greece and Rome, while seeming to presage a science-fiction forum of the future. Perhaps sensing this spiritual aura, the stadium owners take to leasing the arena, off season, to Evangelists and Jehovah's Witnesses. Sometimes a fundamentalist preacher can be heard blaring a call to Christ, which probably goes unheeded in this predominantly Jewish neighborhood.

Diana and I routinely invade any stadium event. We even sneak in when the arena stands empty to sniff up the atmosphere. There are rumors that Jehovah's Witnesses leave a "smell." There is a smell, not unpleasant but distinct. Tropical, like banana. "It's their hair oil," says Diana, an authority on these matters.

Beyond the stadium stands another building almost as magical: the Bronx County Courthouse. This mammoth structure squats, like a granite cake box, on the shelf of the Concourse. It features steep stone steps, for climbing, and larger-than-life-bas-reliefs. We walk, sidewise, a hundred feet above the ground, pressed against stone figures, and cling to their carved coiffures for dear life.

There are two parks for Diana and me to explore. The first park is a flat cemented place, with a single attraction: the "Lorelei" fountain, a group of marble mermaids, whose bare breasts are a source of scandal in the area. All the children climb onto these mermaids' laps and rub their cold, bitten nipples. Diana and I often sit in a central seashell and finger the cracks.

The other park is known as the "dark park," for it is heavily wooded, and offers the only true shade in the area. The shade casts a psychic shadow as well.

We hear occasional screams from the foliage, and there are tales of people disappearing in there. Also: many accounts of sexual deviants, who possibly pop in and out of the park between arraignments at the courthouse across the street. Nice people do not go inside the dark park. They sit, sentrylike, on benches at its exposed borders, too frightened to go in.

Diana is the only girl who ventures into the dark park. She dares me to go with her. I never go in without feeling a chill, never leave without experiencing the exhilaration of escape.

Diana shows me the footpaths, natural tunnels, and near caves. We enter the forest as an outdoor theatre: for a few hours of intense entertainment.

There is soon a price to pay for these tense pleasures. One afternoon we are deep in the trance of play. I am the Squaw, storing pods under a heavy-rooted tree. Diana has been scouting the woods for war parties. She creeps back to camp with whispered news: she has spotted a man with "it" out, wandering in agitated circles.

Always high-strung, Diana, on this day, is almost febrile. She has spoken to him, and reports that he will pay us a quarter "*just* to lower our underpants and show him."

I don't want to "show" him. Diana and I are not entirely innocent. We have, in fact, hung upside-down at a grate next to the Concourse Plaza, to peer into the men's room. We have also paid a fat five-year-old boy to pee. (He did, for a dime, in the privacy of a bus shelter.) But we've never been involved directly with an adult male.

Too soon, Diana is back with this sad-sack fellow in tow. Young, pale, wearing rimless glasses. He carries his penis in his hand, as an injured part. Red as a frankfurter (which is what we call it: there's no choice in this neighborhood), his organ appears inflamed from constant friction. He has a tortured, tired expression. He's been out for hours, unable to find relief.

"A dollar," Diana insists, breathless as she states the overcharge. I look at her—we half-expect the man to refuse.

He agrees, in exhaustion, and Diana leads him to the darkest corner of our forest; a primordial place shadowed by evergreen and hemmed in by high boulders. Once in this natural crevice, our pervert drives his own bargain: we have to touch it.

A lesson follows. He demonstrates how to move the foreskin up and down. We do. He throws his head back, in agonized ecstasy, but sporadically turns petulant and delivers critiques in an objective tone: Slower. No. Not that way.

He says I don't do the job as well as Diana. He also expresses bitterness at my refusal to "show."

"Little bitch," he says, in a low, almost inaudible voice. He mutters, as if he were alone. (Maybe this is why grown men molest small girls—for privacy to be themselves without adult witness.)

He becomes increasingly in control of the situation. Diana ducks behind a tree and drops her drawers—for one second—then yanks them up again, demanding the dollar.

Not yet. He has her work on him, while I turn spectator. I

watch what we call the "cream" splatter, lacquering his pants and a nearby boulder. This rock becomes our instant sexual landmark. For years afterward, Diana and I return to study the stone for signs of the event that has taken place.

"A dollar," Diana gloats. We can do anything, go anywhere, buy anything we want. The man slides back into the shadows, and Diana and I race for home. Then I remember a favorite red hat I was wearing (I picture it hanging on a twig) but decide, without knowing why, that it's not worth going back to retrieve.

Diana and I revise our stories, offer each other expurgated versions of what has just taken place. Even though we know the truth, we pretend to accept our respective explanations, which get increasingly elaborate the closer we get to home.

"I didn't really feel his skin," I tell Diana, who had watched me touch him. "I had a leaf hidden in my hand." The leaf, I explain, separated my palm from his skin. Diana's story is even more elaborate and incorporates tree sap that she used to cover her palm, like varnish that sealed her flesh against his.

We spend the dollar on a French luxury ice cream, cherry vanilla, which we eat with the scrutiny of scientists, taking clinical care to excise the cherries and examine them. When my mother finds us bent over the gallon container, she wants to know how we paid for it. We tell tales of finding quarters on the street, exchanging soda bottles for deposits—then admit what happened.

"It's so ugly." I express *de facto* distaste.

"Not always," my mother says in a tone that gives me pause for thought. "When you love a man, it can be the most beautiful thing in the world."

She calls the police, and warns us away from the dark park.

We go back anyway, but do not see "our" pervert again. We glimpse others. They seem to come out at dusk, opening their pants like night-blooming hibiscuses to reveal their pistils. Whenever I see that distant wrist motion, or a pale bobble in the shadows, I run the other way.

Diana takes off in the opposite direction. She works the territory for a profit. Soon she knows the local child molesters, and has regular "arrangements." She knows who's interested: At the corner cigar store, she disappears into a back room, and emerges with a pocketful of silver dollars. One afternoon, after she leaves, the proprietor takes a gun and blows off his head.

Diana does not editorialize. After all, she is five years old.

*W*e find other ways to make money, some not too savory, but still an improvement. On Halloween, we stand in a cardboard carton that had contained a refrigerator, and use it as a fortune-telling booth. For a dime I tell any woman customer that she will fall in love and marry. If the woman already wears a wedding band, I predict my ultimate blessing: she will have babies.

On St. Patrick's Day, we fold green toilet paper into carnations, and sell them as corsages. Occasionally, we have honest enterprises, but more often we lead exciting lives of crime. Diana can sweep through the five-and-dime and emerge with half the jewelry counter. I have a more white-collar approach: I switch the price markers, go up to a sales clerk, and pay—at great discount. At the soda fountain, we slide other customers' change to our place. More elaborately, we wear fake Red Cross outfits, and rattle a can to collect for "charity." We spend everything on cherry vanilla ice cream or *Pez*.

Diana takes me to the "in" watering spot: Cascades, a swimming pool tucked directly under the Jerome Avenue El, the elevated train that roars to a distant graveyard that is the literal end of the line. At Cascades we lie on imported sand, beside turquoise water, and converse between trains. Our entire beach trembles, and we watch the incoming and outgoing subway cars, in lieu of surf. Still, Cascades is glamorous, with Turkish-tiled changing rooms and a sinus-clearing scent of chlorine. The poolside conversations sound as if they take place at the Cap d'Antibes: "Yes, we come every summer. It's so invigorating."

Diana teaches me to play hooky. We skip as many school days as we attend. Most often we appear in the morning, but duck out at lunchtime. Two five-year-olds on the street during school hours are as obvious as fleeing felons. We are always picked up, often within minutes, sometimes after movie-style chases.

One afternoon we head down to the river, to the Terminal Market, where we play hide-and-seek among the fruit crates. This is a desolate stretch of the city, a cement groin tucked under the bridge, where men slam hardballs. Diana and I are conspicuous—

among the hardball set and the longshoremen. A police car appears, and two officers alight. Diana gives the neighborhood war cry: "Chickie shows!" and runs for her life. I run hard, but the first policeman catches me—a literal collar. Diana turns to see, and is seized. I always remember that if not for me she would have escaped. We are driven, in the back of the patrol car, and remanded to the custody of our kindergarten teacher. I could not feel more a felon.

It seems I am forever guilty. At school, I am routinely summoned to the principal's office, not to answer for my crimes but for my background: "Why is your name different from your father's?"

I feel scalded. I don't know. I say so, but feel as if I'm lying. I begin to invent more interesting answers, including one version in which my father is an Indian chief.

After school, on stoops or sitting on the neighborhood statuary, I keep up a running serial, invented for Diana. Diana listens, taking in my tale with licks of ice cream. As the story quickens, so does her ice-cream licking: we synchronize in our excitement.

I confide to Diana of my other life as Deer Girl, and my involvement with the brave, White Eagle. In most episodes, White Eagle is wounded and I must hide him from his enemies, and nurse him back to health. I usually hide him in a romantic spot— behind a waterfall. And in that damp declivity, mysteriously curtained off from the real world, White Eagle and I draw closer. Later, there are trips to the moon, where we are forced to dance naked in a crater, aboil with lava.

"Go on." Diana likes the idea of trips to the moon. She suggests I sell the story to a comic book.

We move from story to stage-acting. In the somnambulance

of summer afternoons, Diana and I often retire to the privacy of 3M, there to sway and whisper of a near-erotic life we live, somewhere, as slaves. . . .

$\mathcal{I}$m not faithful to Diana. During the next three years I also spend time with another friend, Susan, who is her enemy. I see Susan on alternate afternoons, and play out different scenarios but with similar intensity.

Susan is more typical of our neighborhood. Jewish, middle-class, she lives in AnaMor Towers, in 2L, a junior four apartment that her mother cleans with ferocity. Her mother, Mrs. Hassan, is the fiercest sort of housewife—married to the house, not the man. Her husband, Mr. Hassan, seems incidental: a butcher who works long hours at his distant store, and who, when home, is restricted to his recliner.

We are all forced to walk the plastic paths that cover the well-traveled routes of the Hassan home. If one takes a false step onto the wall-to-wall carpet, Mrs. Hassan will fly at you, murder in her eyes. She is endlessly vigilant. She ignores all social conversation, concentrating instead on where you set down a glass, or if you use the coaster.

Mr. Hassan is dark, his brows heavily inked in the ancestral Cyrillic script. They are Sephardic Armenian Jews. He casts a benign shadow from his corner of the living room. From his recliner he tosses us quarters, and often he sings Sephardic songs, while his wife patrols the rooms scouting for lint. Mrs. Hassan is incongruously pale: a pink-eyed blonde, almost albino.

Susan, their youngest child, is a velvety beauty, black-haired, black-eyed, with Mediterranean skin that seems shaded by maroon blood. She has entered life unwanted, as her mother often reminds her: "I had my family: two grown children. You were an accident." Mrs. Hassan talks about Susan's conception: "I had nothing to do with it: I was asleep."

Perhaps because of the circumstances of her birth, Susan's mother has made only temporary arrangements for her—Susan's place is none too secure. She sleeps in a narrow bed, wedged at an odd angle in her parents' bedroom.

Susan is two years older than I am, and an aeon more mature. By the time she is ten she already has pointy breasts, which other neighborhood girls accuse her of "setting" on bobby pins. Her breasts (more like breast buds) are often on display, featured in Susan's ongoing theatricals, which involve her parading naked for a character known only as "The Sailor."

She will have nothing to do with the Sioux. She doesn't want to know about Deer Girl, White Eagle, or their enemy, Yellow Hawk. Susan is strictly interested in The Sailor, and she is as fierce in fantasy as her mother is in keeping house.

When no one is home in her parents' detergent-scented apartment, Susan leads me to the mint-green quiet of the master bedroom, and demonstrates how her parents' bed splits apart in obedience to Jewish law. During "forbidden" times, the bed must part, sending Mr. and Mrs. Hassan off in opposing directions. There is a secret seam, at which the bed can split. Susan instructs me to "ride" one bed, while she takes off on the other. She operates the bed with a remote control, and, all the while, incants her sexual knowledge in tones reserved for obsessive afternoon encounters. Susan mouths the "have to's" of the true obsessive: "We *have to* be here. . . . We have to turn off the light. . . . We have to lower the blinds. . . . We have to . . . We have to . . ."

At some point, "we" becomes an even more insistent "you" and it's "You have to . . ."

What I have to do is become The Sailor. Following orders, I climb out Susan's window, hang from the fire escape, and peek through her Venetian blinds. Cast as The Sailor, I have to spy on Susan as she undresses.

Susan strips with the slow precision worthy of a professional. Wearing Mrs. Hassan's mink stole over a full slip, Susan eases a strap off one shoulder, then the other. Then she executes a routine with body lotion: applying the cream so that her already pointed breasts become even more noticeably aimed at the window, where The Sailor watches. . . .

At a hand signal, I climb in. Susan lowers her eyes, crosses her hands over her breasts. Oh, this is such a surprise. With half-closed eyes, she maintains a low murmur of dissent: No, The Sailor must not touch her. No, not because she doesn't want him to . . . she does . . . but because this action will cause The Sailor to become "hard" (a condition Susan believes is irreversible). "I don't want you to be embarrassed in front of the other men," she whispers in my ear.

We play by Susan's rules, a constrained courtship for The

Sailor. The Sailor can lie on her mother's bed, as long as he doesn't try to close the distance to the bed where Susan lies, stroking her mink stole, and raising and lowering her legs.

During these sessions, Susan recites her version of the facts of life: When a man becomes hard, he remains that way for the rest of his life. When he wants to have children, he rubs himself naked against his wife's edges. Susan is always anxious to stress that at no time does any part of the man go "inside." "He just *smudges* around the edges."

Susan has a temper, perhaps inherited from her mother, who is known to throw plates. If I balk at entering a Sailor scenario, Susan screams that I'm "a baby" and she can no longer play with me. Once I say, "Okay, I want to play with Diana, instead," and Susan seizes my long hair and holds it in the running blades of an electric fan, until I'm yanked almost fatally forward.

There's jealousy in me, too, but not toward Susan. My courtship is conducted with my mother, and as we settle into our new life at AnaMor Towers, our romance in 3M suffers a few setbacks. Initially, we enjoy a mother-daughter idyll. On Saturday mornings we play ritual gymnastics. I bounce onto her bed, and balance, upside-down, my palms against her knees. This game recalls, fuzzily, an earlier connection. Sometimes, she looks deeply at me, and says in a private voice: "You have his eyes."

She still mentions Larry but he is definitely in the past tense. She buys look-alike dotted-Swiss dresses so that she and I can match. Looking as pretty as possible, we scout the neighborhood. She points out handsome men, as if they are sight-seeing attractions: "There's one . . ."

We make regular pilgrimages on Saturday and Sunday. These excursions remind me of the time we searched for an apartment. Now we are looking at men.

My mother has a kind of wanton shyness on these outings. A tall woman, dressed to the nines, she has a come-hither quality, until a man actually comes hither. Then she turns shy and looks away. She sets up a screen of propriety only a bold man would break.

For weeks, we stake out the tennis courts that are also under the Jerome Avenue El. Again, the country-club atmosphere is regularly punctuated by the urban subway rattle.

"Look, there's one. . . ."

A handsome man in tennis whites: "Curly, the Mayor of Jerome Avenue."

On six consecutive Saturdays, my mother and I watch Curly slam his way to victory in men's singles. After his last match, trophy in hand, Curly approaches our bench. My mother, having stared at him for weeks, now looks down at her dotted-Swiss lap. Curly tells her he likes her smile.

Everyone likes my mother's smile; it eclipses the shadows in her eyes. She is a nice-looking woman with warm brown eyes and a good figure, but she is a beauty on the basis of her smile alone. During the war, she worked for Thornton Wilder, and she has a note from him that thanks her for her smile.

I sulk through her date with Curly. When he looks at me, our enmity is instant, and understood. Curly takes us to a marina at a decayed edge of the city. There, at a café, my mother extols the "sea air," and I dig in a planter with my spoon. I overhear Curly whisper in my mother's ear: "Can't you leave her home?"

The next Saturday night, she leaves me with a baby-sitter, for the first time. We are set up with cookies, coloring books, and clay. I kiss my mother goodbye, but she is gone no longer than five minutes before I throw a floor-pounding tantrum.

How can she leave me for Curly?

We have a game we play, my mother and I. If she walks faster and gets ahead of me on the street, she will always turn to "wait up." If I linger, and can't catch up, she somehow knows this, and retraces her steps to rejoin me.

It's understood that if I am hurt, or need her, I have only to concentrate and call her name, "Rosie," and she'll come running from any distance. I've invoked this charm several times, and it has never failed. Once, when I fell four blocks from home, she somehow heard me, and magically appeared.

Now, thwarted, I sob and overturn our two cots. The blood rushes to my head, and I yowl with the full force of my seven-year-old being: "Rosie."

She returns, moments later, to find me feverish, flattened against the wall.

She stays home on Saturday nights after that. (Poor woman, I ruined her social life.) She seems happy, though—she is a woman who seems to savor every second. We make a game of domesticity; we can dance while we sweep.

Our household flourishes. Pink café curtains wave in the windows. Flowers bloom on the sill. A blue baby parakeet (guaranteed to talk, or your money back) chirps and chatters near our new Emerson radio, which always seems to play. My mother sings, too, songs of lost love, but with a lilt: " 'Twas on the Isle of Capri that I found her. . . . He wore a plain golden ring on his finger. . . ."

And a song that mentions my name: "Hi, Lily, hi, Lily . . . hi . . . *Lo* . . . a song of love is a sad song, don't ask me how I *know* . . ."

Unlike Mrs. Hassan, who cleans all the time with fierce distaste, my mother cleans very seldom (we have so few possessions our studio is intrinsically neat), but she cleans as if it were some sensual sport. She applies lemon-scented polish with wide, graceful motions. My mother has the talent of making the mundane a delight.

She seems in constant motion. I can never recall her still.

One thing she can't do is cook. She burns hamburgers every night, and in the morning I wake to the sound of her scraping the toast in the sink. We enjoy terrible meals together. At age five, I start to take over. I can cook tomato soup and chocolate pudding, if I stand on a chair by the stove. She becomes so ecstatic when I serve her that soon I try to have something cooking every night when she comes home. She, for her part, always seems to fly through the door with some new treat: the greatest, a pure white kitten, in a cardboard box, who pokes her paw through the air holes.

Like lovers, we exchange surprise gifts: costume jewelry and cologne. On weekends we want adventure, and she always takes me somewhere new: the beach, Central Park. We seem to have a permanent picnic in ever-changing locations.

At night, we write love letters, and I draw pictures of her as a mermaid: "Oh, to be a mermaid fair, sitting alone, combing her hair, with a comb of pearl, and her little girl."

In the morning, she leaves me lunches and love notes: "You love canned pears and I love you." One lunchtime I come home to find my standard sandwich (peanut butter and jelly) and a more serious message: "You looked so lovely this morning, and so kind."

*T*he inclusion of "kind" causes me to worry about her. She needs someone to be kind. Is there someone who isn't kind? What's wrong?

Nothing, she says, but we begin to spend the occasional Saturday afternoon in a doctor's waiting room. I hear a word I don't know: "anemic." But my mother has such high color. She runs as fast as I do. One night, after work, she takes me to a bicycle store, buys me a blue bike, and races alongside me as I pedal for home. And she wins.

On one visit to the doctor's waiting room, I see a woman unbutton her blouse and nurse her baby: a first. Did I ever do that? No, I was bottle-fed. Was it long after, and can this be true? I am now seven years old, sitting on her lap in the sunlight streaming in our window, and I bury my head under her blouse.

Do we sense how soon our life together will end? There are nights in our small apartment when I hear her cry, on her side of the el. We now have our beds arranged for privacy. She sleeps against the long wall; I'm around the corner on the short side. Although not in sightlines, we often speak in the middle of the night. "Rosie?" "Lily?" "Are you all right?"

One Sunday she suggests a special outing: a rowboat ride around Central Park. She rows hard, smiling, singing, then we take a walk together in the Ramble. It seems even darker in there than in the dark park.

Rosie stops, stretches out our blanket. She lies down to rest. I charge on ahead, announce: "I'm going to the happy hunting grounds," and within seconds I'm lost.

I wander across some psychic border, into another world: a natural amphitheater, dank and dark. I know at once that I will never find my way back. I stop, call: "Rosie," and, a moment later, she materializes beside me.

The next day she prepares me for school. She helps me dress: neatly pressed white blouse, clean pink skirt, matching socks, and mary janes. As she braids my long hair, I feel her fingers pause: "I should have shown you how to do this for yourself." She asks me to try. I try to work my hair into complicated plaits, but fail. I leave for school, with a crooked part and a tiny tug to the left.

My keys are pinned to my blouse pocket. When I come home, it is not to wait for Rosie but for her younger brother, Gabe. He's to watch me until she can come home in "a few days."

At thirty-eight, Uncle Gabe is still called "the kid" in the family. He looks twenty years younger. ("What's your secret?" relatives ask. "Nonliving," he answers.) No longer a boy, but still boyish, adulthood still somehow up ahead, Uncle Gabe doesn't come at life head-on, but dodges in, as if in a pickup game of basketball: always looking up in expectation, the light glancing off his glasses, moving forward on the balls of his feet. Often his hat falls off behind him.

In the family it is said Gabe "doesn't notice much—his head is in the clouds." He accepts this criticism as complimentary: "In the clouds? Oh, thank you. I try."

Gazing skyward, Gabe always seems slightly abstracted, as if alternately alarmed and amused by his secret thoughts. Fleeing public opinion that he should "settle down," Uncle Gabe takes the streets running. When he picks me up at school, we race a zigzag course toward home. . . .

Where is Rosie?

Uncle Gabe walks me to the hospital—some ten blocks away, on a slanted street, near a stone staircase. I am not allowed inside. Too young. I sit, stewing, on the steps. I fear for Rosie, but I project only my own fears. I'm terrified that she will be forced to undress, that the doctors will see her naked. On the phone Rosie reassures me: that hasn't happened.

"Don't let them see you," I advise.

"The doctor is very handsome," she reports.

I try to slip past the nurse to get up to her room, and I'm caught. "I'm twelve," I lie.

"You're not," the nurse says, putting me outside.

I squeeze my eyes and concentrate: "Rosie."

A window, ten stories above, opens, and Rosie—her curly black hair, a pink nightgown—appears. "Lily," she calls. "Here. Catch."

A tiny square object falls to the pavement. I pick it up and see: it's a tightly folded dollar bill. My allowance. I run at once to the corner drugstore and try to buy her favorite perfume. "Fleur de Lys" is beyond me, and I keep saying "Floor Dilly, Floor Dilly," until they sell me a bottle of something.

At home, Uncle Gabe's first action is to change the sleeping arrangements. He tests my mother's daybed, and pronounces it "too soft." He immediately phones for a superfirm mattress and a bedboard too. He pushes the bed farther down the wall, closer to the door.

I lie in my bed, around the corner of the el and listen to ominous sounds of change. It's strange having him here. A new presence disturbs the night air. I creep around the corner and peek:

Uncle Gabe is a more formal sleeper than my mother: Rosie slept in the nude, or in pink nightgowns. Uncle Gabe lies fully attired in maroon pajamas, his eyeglasses and a prayer book on the floor beside him. He starts out as a rigid sleeper, lying straight on his back, but as the night wears on he relaxes: even the elastic of his pajamas relaxes—the bottoms droop and flash a half-moon of white flesh. He has rolled onto his side, and every so often he moans or clears his throat. Religious even in unconsciousness, he occasionally groans: "Oh God."

At dawn he rises and sways instantly into prayer. His shadow plays across "my" wall. In his striped *tallis,* with multiple head bindings, he presents an apparition at 6 a.m. Observant Jew that he is, Gabe would be unhappy to know that to me he appears to be . . . an Arab.

I know Uncle Gabe but not well. We have had a few afternoons when he has minded me in the past. He has one strong suit: he plays as savagely as a child. He invents his own games. Birdie and the Giant is one. He swoops down after Birdie, and I dive under the bed.

The next night, our first full evening together, I teach Uncle Gabe how to cook my favorite foods. Gabe is curiously ignorant in this area. Later, I learn he cannot identify particular foods even when he is eating them. "Oh, fish," he will say, while spooning in potato salad. Or, "Pumpernickel!" while eating a piece of flank steak. There's no explanation for Uncle Gabe's peculiarity in this area. In the family they simply say, "Gabe doesn't know what he eats."

He's an eccentric at marketing, as well. He appears never to have purchased food. We go to the local superette, and I (taking wild advantage) claim my mother wants us to eat a great deal of ice cream. Instead of buying a standard pint of ice cream, Uncle Gabe manages to find a box of "powdered ice cream" (perhaps a leftover from World War II). We then go back to 3M, and painstakingly prepare this mix. I am not a great deal of help, and when the curds form in an unappetizing sea of yellow fluid, I say: "I don't understand: I followed all the destructions."

And Uncle Gabe roars. He laughs the way he plays: totally out of control, doubling over, until his hat falls to the floor. His next panic is more serious. At bedtime, I tell him I always take a bath. In the throes of this gender-related crisis, Gabe telephones an aunt and asks her to advise him. Gabe concentrates, bent over the receiver: "So let me get this straight. . . ." then, totally panicked, he works out a more typical urban bachelor solution: he has the aunt taxi over to run the tap.

The next afternoon, after school, Uncle Gabe is waiting at the Cyclone fence. "Do you want to play?"

Of course. "Show the way," he cries. Uncle Gabe is a songwriter, and he loves a rhyme, no matter how forced. He has rhymed "river" with "liver" in a love song. •

I take terrible advantage of him. Without relating the unsavory past, I lead Uncle Gabe straight to the dark park. "Oh, well, this looks enjoyable." Gabe also writes nature poems (thousands of them), and says he already feels inspired. He takes notes in a spiral pad that he carries in the pocket of his sagging suit. I see the first words he writes: "Through tunnels of gold, we ran a race. . . ."

And so we do. Forsythia is in bloom, and as Gabe cries, "The chase is ON!" I duck under the yellow arches: at six feet one he must stoop and come after me on all fours, but the new game is begun. "The chase is on."

From then on, wherever we are, Uncle Gabe may suddenly announce: "The chase is on" and it *is*. . . .

I leapfrog over boulders, dash down trails, hide in crevasses, but he always looms up over me: The Giant. He runs in his shined street shoes, neatly laced, but Gabe has also played semiprofessional basketball, and he can outpace me. Mostly I try to run and hide. Often all I see of Gabe is those shined shoes, as he stalks the dark park, near but not finding me. . . .

Every afternoon, we race, up and down the footpaths, into

the natural caverns of the park. He runs hard, and I flee in the earnestness of play, believing for that time that The Giant may kill me. My running explains symptoms that are already there: a knock in my chest, sweat at the small of my back. I end up breathing so hard no one could tell it from a sob.

*D*iana steals a present for my mother: a vaguely Indian terra-cotta vase. The vase sits in the grimed window of a gas station, at a border of our neighborhood. This section is in a no-man's-land of highway overpasses, garbage-strewn lots, and condemned buildings. Diana chooses this as a play area, "because it's all ours." We invent a game, utilizing crushed motor-oil cans. We use them as platform shoes: by scrunching the centers, we can wedge our feet in and clamber a few inches above the oil slick underfoot. "We are giants," she announces.

On her motor-oil-can wedgies, Diana approaches the garage attendant, a man covered in oil himself, and offers her "life savings," a dollar, for the vase. When he refuses, she waits till dusk, then reaches in the window. The vase is dispatched, via Uncle Gabe, to my mother, who "can't get over" how pretty it is.

Diana and I have our own construction project at the edge of a demolition site. We are building an Alamo to defend ourselves against unspecified but expected attack. We gather blasted bricks and stack them into four walls. The result: a roofless shelter of startling unsoundness. Diana, our architectural engineer, places the rear retaining wall plumb on the edge of a precipice. If we lean back against the wall, we will fall two hundred feet onto the Cross Bronx Expressway.

We beautify the shelter, add decorative items: wildflowers in jelly jars. And we hoard provisions—peanut butter, grape jam, comic books, pillows and blankets, all stolen from home. During the lengthening afternoons of late spring, Diana and I spend increasingly long hours in our fort, working up to the time we will stay overnight, and then live there on a permanent basis.

We both dream of a "private house." Here and there, such houses still remain in the neighborhood: narrow frame buildings squeezed between high-rise AnaMor-like towers. I also have my eye on a construction shack across the street, and have gone so far as to offer the nightwatchman seven dollars (my life savings) as a down payment. The watchman explains that the shack is temporary, and will be torn down when the building is completed. "What a waste," I think, trudging back across the street, "when Rosie and I could live here. . . ."

The fort will have to do—but there are problems: no roof, and, of course, Diana has squatter's rights. And, much as I enjoy Diana, the longer I stay in the fort with her the more uneasy I feel. . . . She does psychological spinarounds. One day, she insists that she be allowed to study my belly button.

In the privacy of our fort, I allow her to examine the belly button, but I find the experience embarrassing and—when she pokes her finger in—slightly painful. Her own belly button (so often displayed) is very different from mine: a protuberant knot, as if too hastily tied, and left sticking out as an afterthought. I connect her belly button with her lower economic status (doctors too overworked and underpaid to finish off the umbilical properly) and her religion (a sign of her Catholicism—a female version, similar to lack of circumcision on a male).

Yet I am drawn to her belly button as she is to mine. Everything about Diana exerts a pull: her blondness, her blue eyes, her dead-white "Christian" skin. In my mind, I connect her to Larry, whose hair was also "white in the sun." When I study Diana, I search for signs of Christianity in myself. I could look at her for hours.

On alternate afternoons I see Susan: I commute from one dream state to the next. I sense Susan is working up to a plot climax. The Sailor is being shipped out, and Susan announces that we are "running out of time." Dictatorial as a Broadway British director, Susan insists we go into a heavy schedule of rehearsal. If I don't enter the bedroom window exactly on cue, she demands I do it over . . . and over . . . again.

It's exhausting and exhilarating. I climb in and out of her parents' window, crying out, "I'm here on leave . . . we only have a few minutes," more times than I can count.

She sprays herself with her mother's atomizer (Tabu) and pouts. "I've been waiting for you."

In 3M, Uncle Gabe is also waiting for me: "I don't know what you do all afternoon."

"Play," I say, in exhaustion.

Uncle Gabe uses his free time to write more songs. He sits at my mother's card table, working on his spiral pads, writing so hard and fast the little table shakes. Writing is a physical act for Gabe: "I have to keep churning it out," he explains. As he works, he drinks glass after glass of hot tea, and mops at the beads of sweat on his brow. He often pauses to wipe his eyeglasses across his shirt front: the lenses cloud, as he works up steam.

Gabe belts his songs out in the shower. I wake to his full volume: "We are standing by the sea, and de-manding to be free. We were born in misery. . . ." Although a religious Jew, many of his songs are gospel, and he sings with either a black intonation or a country-western twang. Other tunes are love songs in an Irving Berlin tradition (often with an Irving Berlin melody): "Love is a river . . . flowing for-ever, while by your side I stumble a-long. . . ."

Gabe confides that all his songs are inspired by girls he has loved, and who, for whatever reason, have not loved him. Unrequited passion is the force that propels Gabe along: "While by your side I stumble a-long. . . ."

Some of his songs strike me as self-deprecating: "I'm not certain of nothing, as I get up each morning. . . ."

Gabe often works until midnight, or later, and I might be

jarred from a sound sleep by a sentiment such as: "I've been look-ing for an on-de-level la-dy. . . . Dis one's fat an' dis one's small. . . . And dis one's dat and dis one's tall."

He expects to "hit the big time": a bandleader in a Miami Beach hotel once played "Love Is a River" to a dinner crowd who "went wild." Until then, he has to keep "churning it out" be-cause, as he puts it, he has ". . . a yearning, burning."

He has a stack of sheet music as tall as I am, but Uncle Gabe makes his actual living teaching library science in the basement of a private school in Manhattan. The school is housed in a gray stone mansion, where his library is given short shrift: "They put me and the books in a converted toilet."

Gabe takes me there. It's true. His library has a slanting tiled floor, and Gabe stands, intoning the Dewey Decimal System, with a drain at his feet.

I have no clear idea where Uncle Gabe lives when he is not staying with me. Somewhere in Brooklyn, in a rented room, near an orphanage. He never returns there, but always comes home to 3M, where I have Rosie's mattress propped against my wall, in anticipation of her return.

Yet the "few days" stretched to two weeks, and still Gabe is with me, and there is no definite return date set for Rosie, al-though Gabe says she is "making a wonderful recovery."

My gifts and new poems and pictures are smuggled up to Rosie by Uncle Gabe. "Dolling," I write to her (in the accents of AnaMor Towers), "don't cry: You'll be all right, by and by." Diana and Susan put aside their enmity, in a fit of crayoning sym-pathy, and give me drawings of red roses and their scrawled mes-sages: "Get well, Roses . . ."

Rosie, from her hospital room, continues to send me gifts. I open the mailbox one afternoon, and find a raccoon cap: "Davy, Davy Crockett . . . King of the Old Frontier . . ." I wear it until my forehead sweats.

Rosie writes to me, and we talk every night on the phone. Her voice is the same: a cheery crackle. When she gets out of the hospital, we will go straight to the beach. I harp on my main fear: "Have the doctors seen you naked?"

She laughs: "Not yet."

Then there comes an afternoon when I run into Gabe on the street. He is walking slowly from the El: he's been to see my mother. I rush to him and lead him to a store window to point out a miniature dish set. Such campaigns are successful with Rosie. "Lily has champagne tastes," she says, whenever I waltz through Woolworth's.

Whatever my taste, I can go unerringly to the most expensive item in a store. This dish set, I know, is an incredible luxury item (a $5 dish set), but it features a miniature cooking pan and a tiny Campbell's soup can. There's nothing I admire so much as an object reduced to child size: I have built whole cities in my mother's planter.

"Now?" Gabe looks shocked. "You want a five-dollar dish set, *now?*"

I burn with shame. Of course, not *now,* not with Rosie still away in the hospital. On purpose, I try to recover by asking in a deliberate, grown-up tone: "Oh, by the way, how's Rosie?"

Gabe changes color, plants his feet, braces his body, and begins to shout. "Oh, *by the way?*" he screams, turns on his heel, and leaves me standing in Yogi Berra Plaza.

I walk to the oil-slick section, don my crushed motor-oil-can shoes, and clomp out my fear. Do I know then, that afternoon, what is really happening?

But that night is normal. I teach Gabe how to prepare chocolate pudding from the box. He concentrates, learns to watch for the thickening. When we sit down to eat, he produces a surprise gift: the dish set.

The first day of summer, 1955. The school term is almost over, and Susan and I have been let out early. I've run home as usual, to the deserted 3M, to play. The phone rings. It's Gabe: I should go down to the Hassans' apartment and stay with Susan overnight.

Unprecedented. I have never slept in a strange home. I don't want to sleep down there, in 2L, with Them.

At dinner Mrs. Hassan is critical: "You don't eat the real food, but you like the sweets, don't you?" I fear their foreign food, the alien etiquette in their dinette. And, indeed, the table, set for four (Susan has a much older brother, Aaron, handsome save for a scar on his cheek, where his mother struck him with a plate), is a Formica gauntlet for me to run. Mrs. Hassan has positioned an extra chair, unlike the others, at a sharp corner of the table. I have to fit into their family at an odd angle, a draft at my back.

After dinner, I'm assigned to share the narrow bed allotted to Susan, next to the window (where by day I am ordered to climb in). Mr. and Mrs. Hassan lie down into an instant sleep in their divided bed: This must be a forbidden time. Their beds have split at the seam, and they lie aimed away from one another. In the dark they look like the sarcophagi that Diana and I study when we invade Egyptian museum exhibits.

I look out the window to see the street metamorphose. The sidewalks have turned white and are giving off a malignant sparkle, as if rhinestones have been ground into the pavement. I have never seen the street at 3 a.m. before—it seems covered by an out-of-season snow.

Inside the bedroom, two floor-model fans generate artificial breezes that make the curtains blow. My top sheet billows above my head. I bury my face in a Hassan pillow, but suffer only a body-twitching recall to consciousness, which shows how far I can fall.

Beside me, Susan twists, nursing the corner of her pillowcase. Unconscious, she seems to sense need nearby. She pats me twice, as though to say, "Everything will be all right."

Her blind gesture reassures. Yes, everything *will* be all right; it's just the middle of the night.

I wake at dawn to a belly clutch. I won't eat the nutritious breakfast Mrs. Hassan prepares especially for me. I can't wait to escape from them, their food, their alien apartment.

At school the day seems to realign. I sit at my usual desk, do multiplication tables. Study the ear of the boy I love (a blonde from the Ukraine, named Tuchek). He sits in front of me, and I want to bite his white earlobe: will it crease, like a marshmallow, between my teeth? We never speak.

The summer holiday mood prevails—we are let out, whooping and running. Susan and I race back to my apartment to try on new swimsuits and shorts. She will be going to camp soon, and she has brought up her new summer wardrobe to show me. She dons a pair of wide peach-colored shorts, and wants to know: Can boys see up them?

I lie down on the polished floor and look up. I am trying to "see," when I hear the key in the lock. Gabe opens the door, but does not immediately enter. Instead, there is the sound of fumbling in the hall, and he holds the door open with his foot. Then he kicks the door open all the way, and sets a pine bench in the foyer.

Do I know the meaning of the bench? Or why Uncle Gabe is, for the first time, unshaven? Gabe motions to Susan to leave, and she does . . .

I sit up, grasp comfort in Gabe's first words: "Your mother was very sick last night. . . ."

Very sick. I feel relief. Very sick, *not* . . .

"She died."

I run, run from the apartment, down the steps, across the false marble floor, past ceramic murals of fixedly-staring maidens. . . . Run down the street, now hot and sunny, jammed with other mothers, sitting on folding chairs.

They look up as I appear, and I see that they are talking about me. They are speaking in high voices. They seem more excited than I have ever seen them. These women thrive on tragedy. I have seen this before—their sudden stimulation when a police car has pulled up to the lobby door, or when an ambulance has carted someone away from AnaMor.

Mrs. Hassan plays hostess to this event. She stands before the gathering semicircle. She says, with what strikes me as grim satisfaction: "First the father, now the mother . . ." She wonders aloud: "What will happen to her now?"

I run past her in a blur of hate. How can she live? I run to the slum-next-door, take the six flights up to Diana's. I run as fast as I have ever raced . . . through the always-open door to Mrs. Duval, who rises from her easy chair.

She takes me at once into the folds of her body. She begins to cry, tears washing from her faded blue eyes, running down her red cheeks. I feel her breasts shake against me.

A strange response. Her sobbing convinces me the news is not true. It's a joke. In fact, I made it up—and Mrs. Duval believes me. I start to shake, too, as hard as Mrs. Duval, but not with sobs, with laughter I know I should suppress. Why make her feel foolish? How can she believe such a made-up story?

I do a literal about face: turn and run, fleeing down the steps like a spooked cat. I pass Diana, a ball in her hand. Somehow she knows too and chases me in earnest—across the street, through traffic, to the construction site at the brink of our cliff. There, at the precipice, we enter our Alamo and, out of breath, we sit.

We stay, in a silence I appreciate more than words, until after dark. Then, to ward off the chill, we turn and sit back to back. I feel the heat of Diana's bare skin: she wears a halter. We stay there that way, not speaking, but feeling the warmth and support where we lean against one another, until, in total blackness, Diana leads me away. She guides me down the steep stone staircase to my house, where Gabe is waiting, sitting on the new pine bench.

*I*n the social flurry that follows the funeral, neighbors and relatives come and go, carrying coffeecakes. uncle Gabe tells me that it is Jewish custom to bury the dead within twenty-four hours, and that Rosie is already in a grave. Now we are "sitting *shiva*," a period of mourning in which we receive visitors. Because we actually quake on our plain pine bench, I translate this procedure as "sitting shiver."

Only my uncle Gabe, his brother, Len, and I sit "shivering."

Uncle Len has materialized in 3M overnight. He's there somehow in the morning, when I awake with the belly clutch, to the first day of life without Rosie.

He is a startling sight in the predawn dark, sitting on a crate. At six feet six, Uncle Len resembles Abraham Lincoln (and perhaps not so coincidentally has long revered him). In the shadows, dressed in black, Uncle Len appears as an apparition: the Lincoln Monument in 3M.

The mystery of his midnight arrival is consistent with Uncle Len's history: he has long been an enigma to the rest of the family. At forty, he is two years older than Uncle Gabe, and several inches taller, but he casts an even longer shadow. He wears slouch-brimmed hats and heavy trenchcoats, and seems to have modeled himself on a Dashiell Hammett character. He does in fact work part-time as an investigator (though he's characteristically vague as to whom or what he investigates). His personal style seems inspired by an espionage novel: he loves to cover his tracks. He communicates by mail, usually through postcards without return addresses, or through recorded voice tapes, which are mailed, with instructions, to the recipients.

Until this time, my experience with Len has been primarily indirect—although he alludes to having lived with me and Rosie for several months when I was an infant. In fact, he was present at my birth, and never asked Rosie what had happened with my father. "I don't like to pry" is Len's standard answer.

A bachelor, he is himself hounded by questions: Why aren't you married? Do you have a girlfriend? He refuses to answer, and so is too considerate to ask anyone else such a personal question. He is a man who can find his sister nine months pregnant, on the doorstep of his apartment, and not, as he would say, "make any inquiries."

On my birthdays, he always mails voice tapes, or, on occasion, handmade records, with instructions as to when and how they should be played. On the assigned night, Rosie and I would sit by our bakery birthday cake and listen to Uncle Len's prerecorded message. He speaks in a soft voice, but weighs his words with Gettysburg intensity:

"We are gathered here today, on the twenty-fifth of January to celebrate the seventh birthday of Lily Pearl . . . In honor of this event . . ."

Uncle Len at that moment would appear in our L-shaped studio, with a package that he would imply came from the Orient or Latin America. His usual preamble: "I am not at liberty to say where this item was acquired." He would offer hints: he has recently visited the "capital of a distant nation," and my birthday present has something to do with "proof of their goodwill." Uncle Len never conducts himself with anything less than an attitude "conducive to international diplomacy." His personal style is that of an undercover president on a good-will mission.

On this night, Uncle Len brings only himself and a change of clothing, packed in a manila envelope. I imagined his odd choice of luggage is because of the emergency situation, that he had no time to pack. (Later, I learn Uncle Len will only travel with manila envelopes—he likes to travel light and also alludes to his "cover." On his "secret" missions, he carries shorts, socks, and his work-in-progress, "the Lincoln biography," in the envelopes.)

For the next seven days, we crouch ragged, unwashed, on the *shiva* benches, to receive condolence callers. Like survivors of a shipwreck, we subsist on their offerings of cellophane-wrapped fruit.

In accordance with another Jewish law, Uncle Gabe takes a serrated blade and hacks off the lapels of his jacket and Uncle Len's. Gabe suggests he slice the sleeve of my blouse, but Uncle Len says, "I don't think that will be necessary," the first of his soft-spoken interventions on my behalf.

Rosie's off-white studio, her hard-won cubicle that was our special place, now turns into an emergency bivouac. My uncles and I sit, quite still, on the pine *shiva* seats. The only sign of levity is my white cat, Sparkle, who swings from the rungs of my seat, and uses the new wood as a scratching post. The cat, stimulated by the comings and goings, runs sudden races with herself around the room. In his cage, the blue parakeet continues a constant chatter to his reflection, regurgitating small meals to his mirror self.

Each night Uncle Gabe divides the daybed and gives the top half to Len: "Here, you take the mattress, I'll take the box spring." They lie stretched out, side by side, in the main area of the apartment, while I sleep around the corner, in the short end of the el.

Sleep, always a solace, is now elusive. I waken in the dark, yanked, as if by a crane, from my dreams, to reacquaint myself with what Uncle Len calls "the setup." No one regards the setup as permanent. Arrangements, I hear the visitors whisper, will be made. It is expected that other relatives, more logical candidates than my two uncles, will come and take me.

That thought sends a different shiver through me. At night I lie awake and wonder: Where is Rosie really? During the days, I pretend to believe that she has died, but I suspect the truth is that she has been spirited away, to a secret hiding place. I consider the alternatives—the seashore? the mountains? another hospital? In the courtyard of AnaMor Towers, I have heard tales of people who became "mental" and were hidden from their families for years. "We were told she died" is a not uncommon remark. "Then we *found out . . .*"

Someone is keeping her somewhere, against her will, or it's possible she had amnesia. I tend to envision her being held by force, and brood over where "they" are hiding her. And who are "they"?

I suspect our visitors, with their morbid zest to pay respects. Their relish is so apparent I'm half certain they have engineered the occasion.

The condolence callers come bearing platters and platitudes. They tell me Rosie's in heaven. How I chafe at that. She would never go without me. Their sympathies have a reverse effect: I cringe whenever we have to open the door to admit another overly dramatic mourner. My uncles must share my antipathy: when the buzzer shrills, we all scream and fall to the floor.

"I know how you feel" is the standard greeting. "My great-aunt just dropped dead—just like that, on the dance floor." Our callers are escorted by a legion of their departed grandparents, aunts, cousins, nephews. We are forced to entertain these phantoms, the mordant multitudes: "Two aunts in two days . . . both embolisms. I lost five cousins to cancer in the last ten months."

For many of our neighbors, these statements do not represent much of a departure from their daily style. Their usual social preliminaries often take the form of synopses, which they offer on introduction: "Hello, I lost my husband to a massive coronary after nineteen years. I have one son, a diabetic, and a daughter with a club foot that was, thank God, fixed. My husband invested everything in his business, and when he died, his partner stole everything, and I was wiped out. I don't know how I survive, but I do."

And how do you do?

My uncles are incapable of capsule summations for what has happened here. They hunch on the pine bench, in silence, suffering a grief beyond condolence, while other co-mourners thrive on the scene. Sometimes, during the first days, I think of locking the door against the sympathizers. But that would be impolite, whereas their enjoyment of our situation is well within the etiquette laws of AnaMor.

While a few visitors, pale and shaken, offer true consideration, many more exhibit the secret stimulation of motorists who rubberneck at auto accidents. They interrogate, wanting details to add to their grim relish: "So it had spread?" A favorite comment, not quite whispered, is "I heard when they cut her open she was *riddled* with it. They just closed her right up again."

This emotional terrain is as barren and ugly as our actual surroundings. We live in a Bronx of the emotions, a place where the flats of mediocrity are only relieved by steep descents into hysteria: "Only the good people die!" (Mrs. Hassan). The bad ones, intriguingly, might live forever. I'm offered every cliché of "loss": I'm "lucky" to have had a mother for eight years. I could have had none at all. Now I'm lucky to have a mother in heaven, where she can watch over me.

My mother's death seems to have stimulated entire sections of the borough. One woman, a total stranger, pokes her head in our door and intones nasally: "Oh, I heard and I just had to see. You know I feel sorry for you." We receive Hallmark cards from people whose names we do not even know: a thousand sympathy greetings with print flowers and religious symbols. The cards stand in a tower (and are finally stored in grocery sacks on the floor).

I'm a featured attraction at this show. "That's the little girl." I chafe at their interest in me, so blatantly (and with characteristic delicacy) expressed: "Does anyone know what will happen to her now? Will someone take her or will she be sent to an institution?"

My uncles answer, in low mumbles, "No, no, no . . ." They have the grace to say "hssssh," but the sympathizers are unstoppable. They loudly define what makes this death worse than other deaths: "This one is a young person, with a small child."

And in another delicate move, the mourners love to project tradeoffs: "Why couldn't it have happened to the old man in 2J?"

Why couldn't it?

Meanwhile, I glean overheard nuggets of information: more relatives are expected from another state, a childless aunt and uncle, a married couple, with their own home. "There's another uncle coming, this one's married: They'll take her. . . ."

While we wait for the out-of-state Uncle Norm and his wife, Aunt Barb ("She can't have children, or she doesn't want them?"), more mourners invade 3M. By the third day I start to take stock. I count my mother's dresses—five. They are all accounted for, still hanging in her closet. Ominously, her new peach silk nightgown, purchased for her hospital trip, is now returned, and rests on a stack of her other clothes, near the door. When a visiting neighbor snatches this gown, and holds it to her frame—"My size," she cries—I take the precaution of hiding Rosie's other favorite clothes: her handknit ice-skating sweater, her party dress with the zigzags of bugle beads.

My mother's pink café curtains—hung only weeks before— still flutter in the electric-fan breeze. To me, these curtains are our banners, proclaiming her plans.

She's coming back. She has to.

Her new pink bedsheets are now draped over the mirrors. I see a twin-sized sheet with a flower-sprig pattern hung over the medicine chest, as yet another observance of religious tradition. Uncle Gabe tells me the rule: after someone has died, no one can look into a mirror for one week.

I interpret this to mean: If I look, I die, too. For more hours than I can count I confront that pink percale and debate. . . .

I touch the corner of the bedsheet. If I lift the sheet, do I die instantly, then join Rosie? I half expect, if I raise the cover, I will see her, smiling, in the glass. But what if it's not true? What if I die, and I don't get to go with her? If I could only believe, without doubt, I would lift that sheet, and enter the afterworld of our medicine chest. But even then, at eight, I'm skeptical enough to suspect that I could die and be dispatched to a separate place.

No, it's better to believe she'll return. She said we would go to the seashore or out to the country. She will probably find a way to contact me, or somehow I will find her on my own.

My belief that Rosie is secretly alive anesthetizes me from what is truly going on in 3M. I duck the visitors' questions. And when they try to quiz me on the street, I run.

I run faster than ever: Gabe has bought me new red sneakers. We—my uncles and I—all wear sneakers throughout this week of "shiver." The sneakers are another religious accoutrement of grief. Uncle Gabe explains: "God doesn't want us to wear hard soles." He wants us, it appears, to wear Keds.

In those first dazed days, we suffer other, lesser catastrophes. In the chaos that follows death, my uncles and I wander, disoriented, on our infrequent forays into the outside world. We take wrong buses and trains, walk past familiar landmarks, lock ourselves out of the apartment. First you lose a person; then you lose everything.

My cat, the white kitten Rosie gave me, this little Sparkle, has soon vanished, too, disappearing during the grief traffic in and out of our door. Mewing, Uncle Len, Gabe, and I stalk the corridors. We leave out a dish of tuna fish, but Sparkle is not seen again. Uncle Len comforts me by saying that surely someone has admired Sparkle's beauty and snatched her for themselves. Again I regard the neighbors with suspicion. Is my cat held hostage behind their doors?

It's said that deaths occur in a series—that one death begets other deaths. And this holds true in 3M. One morning, Uncle Len lifts the birdcage cover and cries out, "Don't look."

I rush past Uncle Len to see him: Skippy, upturned, his claws curled to his blue chest—a mystery fatality on the sandpaper floor of his cage. It's too terrible to contemplate. Did we, in our distraction, forget to feed him and change his water dish? Or, following Uncle Gabe's religious doctrine, did Skippy break with Orthodox observance, while sitting "shiver" on his perch? We had not forgotten to feed him, it turned out—there was millet among the chaff—but we had forgotten to cover his mirror.

While I have been excluded from my mother's funeral, I take an active role in the parakeet's. Skippy is placed in a small pouch that once held Uncle Len's pipe tobacco. Diana and I carry him, in the pouch, to a shaded spot in the dark park, not far from where we had our dealings with the pervert.

While still refusing to believe Rosie is dead, I do not deny what has happened to Skippy. The word "dead" has some meaning to me when applied to birds. One afternoon, in the park, I saw a bulgy-eyed bird embryo, and Rosie herself said, "That's dead."

Len, Gabe, Diana, and Susan stand by at Skippy's funeral, but only I return several days later to dig him up. What suspicion has entered my heart that I have to "see" what is "happening" to him? Fortunately, his remains cannot be located. Either I forgot the exact location, or an animal has made off with Skippy, tobacco pouch and all.

I cry for Skippy, in frustration at not finding him as much as at "the loss." Diana reappears on the scene to offer her version of religious comfort. She leads me to the neighborhood Catholic church.

Inside, I see as if through the garnet-colored votive candles. A carnal gloom. Diana lights several candles, pockets some change from a collection dish, and leads me through what I regard as a chamber of horrors, but which is, according to Diana, a display of "saints being murdered."

In each niche writhes another tortured, life-size statue. Semi-nude, draped in a plaster tunic, each saint has a spear or arrow stuck through the innards. Droplets of blood permanently dribble from each puncture wound. A few martyrs wear simple jewelry, which Diana lifts and stuffs in the pocket of her shorts. All the while, she whispers a campaign to convert me: "Become a Catholic and you get to be a saint. They'll build a statue of you, and you get to see all the other dead people. You're all together in a different place."

Perhaps because I now have Uncle Gabe staying with me, I make a weak attempt to proselytize for Judaism: "Jews put up a whole building in your name."

Diana looks more interested than I do.

We run out of St. Angela Merici, back to the park, where we put on our new necklaces.

When I return, my neck already turning green from St.

Theresa's stolen chains, I find Uncle Norm and Aunt Barb sitting on folding chairs across from Gabe and Len. Norm is their youngest brother, and he appears a shorter, shriveled version of Len. I have heard a story that Norm, when he was three years old, was hit by a car, and has a steel plate in his head. I picture a dinner plate.

Norm has the family eyes—bright and black as espresso beans—but his are reddened and tearing—not specifically for this occasion. Norm always seems to be weeping. He is said to be "allergic."

He is married to Barb, one of the women scissored out of the family album. In the family, most of the in-law women have been regarded as outlaws, representatives of an enemy tribe, who have married "our" men. Barb's vermilion lips and heavy jewelry do nothing to undermine this attitude: She looks every flashy inch the Aztec who is luring her man into an alien, savage society. Barb fits into this scene at AnaMor Towers. She must have walked off the mosaic motif. Her kohl-outlined eyes glare into mine, and I form an immediate feeling as to whether she "can't have children, or didn't want them."

I have heard the family legend that Barb is a worthless "gold digger" who "hooked" Norm when Norm was a lonesome sailor (not The Sailor, apparently) stationed in her southern city, so far from his own real home. What a gold digger would have seen in this near-retarded mechanic was questionable, but I accept on faith a cousin's pronouncement that Barb "grabbed the brass ring." Barb wears large brass hoops through her ears, which lends the legend credence.

Uncle Norm always weeps, even while singing her praises,

"Oh, Barb, Barb is such a wonderful woman. I don't deserve a woman like Barb." His face contorts, reddening, and he sounds overrehearsed. Cousins say, behind his back: "Brainwashed."

His head swiveling in agreement to anything Barb says, Norm does have the look of a POW kept too long in a tin hut. No matter what Barb says—and she's absolutely unquotable ("Yeah, Niagara Falls ain't much. It's just a bunch a water," is a sample remark) —Uncle Norm will nod and add: "Oh, listen to Barb; she's smart: she knows what she's talking about."

When Norm married Barb some ten years before, the marriage was not applauded. Everything about Barb was regarded as suspect. "She gave her age as twenty-two," reports Uncle Len, mimicking a falsetto twenty-two. "Ha, forty-two." Nothing about Barb can be taken on faith. While she claims to be busy around her house all day, Uncle Len points out that her underarms sag. And indeed they do—the underarms hang, bubbling with pocked fat, the consistency of ricotta.

Now she proclaims her grief, squawking in an allegedly southern accent: "Oh, Gad, it's a shame. . . . She was so young. None of us knows when we'll go."

Whereupon, Uncle Norm bobs his head to and fro in another show of senseless agreement: "Oh, Barb's so smart."

Barb and Norm are not new characters to me. Rosie and I once visited their home, a much-valued private house in Baltimore. Barb made us sleep in the living room, on a mohair sofa, without sheets, even though they have a guest room. On investigation, I spotted Norm's shoes under the "guest" bed, and deduced they slept in different rooms.

Now they present a picture of marital solidarity. "I'm so

lucky to be married to Barb," Norm keeps saying, although no one has cued him. Yet he must still have doubts. Periodically, without explanation, he hides his face in his hands.

"We want to do something for Lily," Norm finally says, and Barb shakes her head vigorously, rattling her jewelry.

We all assume they have come to claim me. They are the logical candidates to become adoptive parents. Long-married, childless, with their own home. Other relatives have been beating the Norm and Barb drum, in the background saying, "Barb and Norm will take her: they have the space."

Barb hands me a box, tied with red-and-white-striped string: bakery cookies. "There's more," Barb promises.

I brace myself, to be taken. I look around 3M for the last time. My uncles sit on the pine seats, poised in alarm. As Uncle Norm and Aunt Barb rise to leave, I instinctively move backward, away from them, to sit between my uncles.

Aunt Barb reminds everyone it is a long drive to the city she pronounces as "Bawl-o-more." "But," she says, "we want to do something for Lily. . . ."

Uncle Len clears his throat, but before he can speak, Aunt Barb announces her intention—to take me not to "Bawl-o-more" but to the nearest department store. There, instead of adopting me as their own child (as the chorus of AnaMor had predicted), Uncle Norm and Aunt Barb buy me a blue jumper, with a pink checked blouse. Once dressed in this ensemble, I am returned to 3M, and Uncle Len and Uncle Gabe.

Uncle Norm backs out of 3M, a ward of his bride, who is intoning: "You all come see us, you hear?" Her voice rises to such a screech Len, Gabe, and I flinch, and involuntarily resume our seats. Uncle Norm's face, always brick-red, becomes even redder, and tears of "allergy" stream down his cheeks. He backs out into the hall and into his bride's southern accent: "You all come see us, you hear?" The door closes on them repeating, "Hear? Hear?"

Inside, Gabe, Len, and I breathe a collective sigh. "Now it can be said," announces Uncle Len. "I was quaking."

*A*fter the visitors depart, Uncle Len, Gabe, and I are alone together in a new way. That night I hear them whisper around the corner of the el, from their palletlike arrangement on the floor. They trade questions without answers: "Do you think they would let two O.B.s have her?" I don't know who "they" are, but I know "two O.B.s" is family shorthand for "two old bachelors." "What do you think, Shaine?" says Gabe, who always calls his brother by his last name in times of crisis.

I'm too young and have been too much loved by Rosie to grasp the magnanimity of my uncles' continued presence in the apartment. Of course, they want to stay with me. Although Mrs. Hassan has a new theme: "They should turn her over to the authorities."

The authorities. The word makes my heart hammer as it did when I fled the police. Could they scoop me up again and take me off in the patrol car?

My only goal now is to maintain what remains. I hide the costume jewelry I had planned to give to my mother: an ivory heart-shaped pin, with matching earrings. And in other ways I cling to the status quo. When Uncle Len repaints a cabinet, I cry, and say, "No, it must be the color it always was." When they mention finding a larger apartment, I resist. I say only that I want to hang on to this one a while longer, but the truth is that I expect Rosie to return, and want as little changed as possible.

On the street I stay close to Diana and Susan. They have made a temporary truce, because of the tragedy, and will play together—although I am forever "monkey in the middle."

When Susan announces that she is leaving for camp, I am startled. Of course, I should have realized. Have only two weeks passed since I appraised the new peach shorts she had bought for her "summer wardrobe"? Other lives go on. . . .

Susan. Susan. Susan. Her name becomes my mantra. I want to go with Susan. I want to go to sleepaway camp with Susan.

Susan says she too cannot bear to be apart from me. We must go together. I ask my uncles' permission and they agree; it is a temporary solution, of sorts, while they make "new arrangements." But Mrs. Hassan says it is too late—that camp reservations are made years in advance; the desirable Camp Ava is booked.

Mr. Hassan claims influence, however, and he intercedes on my behalf. My uncles, Mr. Hassan, and my mother's friends contribute the required sum—a hundred dollars for the ten-week season. There are distant rumblings from the mountains: Camp Ava's season is indeed set up, the bunkhouses are filled, but, because of the tragic circumstances, space will be created; there will be one more bed, for one more camper. They do, however, need time, and I will have to join Susan a bit later. "Don't worry," says Mr. Hassan. "You won't be far behind."

Technically, I am close behind on the day of Susan's departure—I chase her parents' car up to the Major Deegan highway, screaming and waving, calling, "Susan, Susan, Susan . . ."

And there, in the rear window, is Susan, her black eyes brilliant with tears, her tanned hand reaching out . . . Susan. Susan. With her black hair and brown eyes, she looks, as she vanishes, more and more like Rosie: dark, comforting.

Susan knows Rosie is not truly gone, also. "They're hiding her," she has assured me. Those words and the sanity of her silence have been more solace than all the words of sympathy. I count the days until I can be with her again and say her name before I sleep: Susan. Susan.

When I'm with Susan, the world will be set right. Already I have lain in bed at night, willing time backward: "Please let it be January again." The crisis can still be reversed, Rosie can yet be restored to me.

Every day, I invoke a new charm. As I approach AnaMor Towers, I walk only on the curb, or I skip every crack on the pavement. I eat only foods that Rosie and I have eaten together (which limits my main-course menu to burned hamburger, hot dogs, tuna croquettes, and cheese omelets).

When I wake in the morning, I squeeze my eyes shut, and will her to reappear on her side of the studio. I count my steps each time I approach the door to 3M from the outside and picture an entire scene inside: Rosie, reading by a lamp, or waltzing with the broom.

So far, none of this has had an effect, but I hold the last charm, the most potent charm, in reserve. If I call her name aloud, she will have to reappear. If I really *need* her, as I have on those other occasions—when I screamed from a street four blocks away, when I was lost in Central Park. In a real emergency she has never failed to materialize. A true cry for help will not go unheard. Yes, she will come when I give the ultimate call. We are playing some extreme game of hide-and-seek. Sometimes, I even whip open my closet door to catch her, but I know that I must save the secret summons, save the most certain charm for last.

I have hopes for the trip to the country, for that seems like a place where she may be kept hidden. She always loved the mountains and forest. Perhaps she's been uncharacteristically inconsiderate, and simply started her vacation and is waiting up there for me. No, I doubt that. Wherever she is, she was taken by force.

As soon as it can be arranged, I'm registered for Camp Ava. There is still something vague said, on the phone, about "finding a bed," but Uncle Gabe leads me on a round of preparations. He takes me to shops recommended by Mrs. Hassan to buy the required camp clothes.

At the store, I discover Uncle Gabe knows even less about children's clothes than he does about his own. (He always wears out-of-style, ill-fitted, saggy suits, with beaten straw hats and mismatched ties and shirts.)

He is my innocent victim in wardrobe selection: I want to look older, so I insist we buy size ten—two full sizes too large. I model enormous shorts and tee-shirts that hang to my thighs.

Neither of us knows they don't fit. We leave, in satisfaction, at having bought "everything."

Next, we visit a tailor who will sew in name tags, decreed a must for camp life. Again I suffer an interrogation: what *is* my last name anyway?

The tailor, a man bent over an ancient sewing machine, says, "I can't leave blank."

Uncle Gabe comes up with the right answer (and a prophetic one, at that): "Give her mine."

And so, off I go, as Lily Shaine.

Uncle Gabe escorts me to camp.

I have campaigned so hard to win this trip that I am the last to admit, when it's time to get on board the bus, that I have a seizure of doubt. Somehow, with my eight-year-old reasoning, the moment of departure had never seemed real: what had mattered was winning permission to go.

Do I really want to leave my block? Uncle Gabe and Len? Diana? I caused so much fuss I have to go. . . . We board a bus with other passengers escaping from the city heat, the softening asphalt.

The second we pull out on the open road, Uncle Gabe gets what he calls "motion sickness." His nausea is profound. He doesn't like changes (although, paradoxically, he often suggests trips). He vomits at fifteen-minute intervals during the two-hour bus ride. We arrive at a mountain hamlet, aptly named High Cragsdale, and are taken by taxi, with Uncle Gabe retching out the window, to Camp Ava.

Camp Ava is weirdly situated, on a mountainside that seems too steep to support its few wooden structures: the entire camp, including the CAMP AVA sign, seems to list downslope and to the left. (This turns out to be symbolic of its political nature as well: the camp was founded and is run by Socialist labor-union leaders.)

We arrive in the pink of sunset: Uncle Gabe and I. He carries an overnight bag, and I drag a pillowcase, packed by Uncle Len: "A pillowcase is a lot like a duffel bag," Len said, the first of his equations that turn out not to work in my social life. "Look," someone whispers. "She doesn't have a suitcase. All she has is a pillowcase."

Clutching the pillowcase, I cross a balding grass lot to a flat building marked OFFICE. As Gabe and I walk (he is already extolling the glories of the country air, in typical urban style—gulping until he hyperventilates), a horn blast stops us in our tracks: "Everybody to the Social Hall."

Dozens of uniformed boys and girls, wearing green-and-white Camp Ava tee-shirts, appear from a ring of white shacks, and move *en masse* to the main building. As I scan this crowd for the longed-for Susan, I catch, in my peripheral vision, a scene I edit from my immediate consciousness. What I see makes no sense, and is too frightening to contemplate.

I will review the scene later—the little girl, naked and silent, scampering across the yard: a flash of pink. She is moving so fast I can doubt having seen her.

The naked girl suggests that my worst fears can be fulfilled here. The uniformed girls are not reassuring as they file past, pointing at me. The rearrange themselves, grouped according to bunk, on the lawn.

I have arrived on the seventh day of a ten-week season. It

might as well have been the seventh century. It's too late. The tribal status of each bunkhouse is already defined. Bunkmates and friendships have been sealed in blood. Enmity and war have been declared between rival bunkhouses, named for flowers. "I hate all Bluebells," I overhear. Then: "They're not as bad as Violets."

I search the crowd for my one familiar person, and there she is: with her cap of cropped hair, golden face, her famous pointy nipples outlined under an Ava tee-shirt: Susan.

She is walking arm-in-arm with a pink sunburned blonde, who appears too plump in her Ava shirt and shorts. Susan spots me. She recognizes me, but appears a bit vague, as if she does know me but is not certain from where.

"Susan?" I ask.

Susan runs to me, her arms open to give me an embrace, but a man with a whistle around his neck comes between us. He is a great bulk of a man—a brisket wearing Bermudas. Even his face is the color of corned beef as he reddens with rage.

"Get back" are his words of welcome.

Manny Rubell runs the camp with the same spirit in which he conducts his garment manufacturer's union during an unpopular strike. He orders Susan back to her line and confronts Gabe and me: "What are you doing here? It's after hours. No visitors."

Uncle Gabe, relentless in his politeness, no matter how rude the proceedings, begins a formal introduction: "Hello, I'm Gabe Shaine, and this is my niece . . ." Manny interrupts him: "Go see Ava first." Nodding, his mouth open in an "Oh" of assent, Gabe leads me, as instructed, to the founder of Camp Ava—Ava.

Ava, arms folded, stands at the entrance of the Social Hall. She seems ancient, a gypsy crone in her paisley skirt and cherry-pit necklaces. Her features are heavy, as if whittled from wood.

Ava has some relationship to Manny, perhaps romantic. In certain aspects, they seem to have switched sexes: Manny has breasts that bobble under his tee-shirt, sliding off to each side, and Ava has whiskers. Her whiskers sprout singly, above her lip and below her chin. Her whisker hairs show more vigor than the gray hair on her head, which is thinning. And, when Ava speaks, a male voice emanates from her, barking commands, giving authoritative grunts. "Light," she says, holding up her cigarette toward Manny. In turn, for all his heft, Manny has a high, light voice that squeaks from him in a steady whine of double negatives that stress the impossibility of my situation.

"I don't know nothing about this one," Manny introduces me. "Where are we supposed to put her?"

As I stand, twisting the corner of my packed pillowcase, Uncle Gabe recites the details of the registration procedures we followed "in the city."

What do they know down there? It turns out "they don't know nothing, neither." Manny escalates to triple negatives in his exasperation with "the situation." The camp is filled. There is no bed.

Ava takes a drag on her cigarette, looks at me through the smoke. She makes sounds too, officially affirmative "yeah, yeah," but expressed with the same negative tone. She has, she says, seen it all before. . . .

Blue-green light suffuses the campground, cosmetizing the shabbiness of the structures. A piny scent fills the air, and an electric chitter-chatter sounds from the high grass. I squint, trying to align the real Camp Ava with my imagined Camp Ava. That camp, a Hansel-and-Gretel-styled forest, complete with rippling brook and gingerbread cottages, is so real to me I cannot quite acknowledge that it doesn't exist. I had so completely envisioned the place that I feel it must be somewhere . . . maybe on the other side of the mountain, or perhaps on another planet altogether. I store the image of my original camp to examine later, and try to accept what I see before me in the growing dark.

Manny and Ava complete a chorus of disgust and disapproval for camp "management" people in the city. "They don't know nothing. They don't know what we have to deal with up here." At last Manny marches off, leading his flock, all the campers, paired off, in buddy system, double file toward some communal "fun."

Ava gives me a hand chop, then a follow-me crook of her fingers. She leads me to a bungalow, no more than twelve feet square and identifiable, by the gypsy skirts, slung drying over a pipe, as her own abode.

She snaps open a folding metal cot, slams it in place, and tosses a thin mattress, with Rorschach-styled blots, on top. "Just for tonight," she says. "I can't sleep with a presence in my room. If I wanted a presence in my room I would have stayed with my husbands."

I know what she means by "a presence."

She yanks open the window beside my cot. The window frames a bough, hung with ripe red cherries. "You will want to reach out and pick those cherries," Ava predicts. "Don't do it. I know how many are there."

That night I lie awake, too aware of the strangeness of these surroundings and the presence of Ava to sink into the solace of sleep. There must be trust—or complete exhaustion—to let one's guard down, to feel safe enough to exhale the vapor of the soul. . . .

The sleeping Ava emits an odd series of sounds: lip smacks and grunts. Once she barks, "Don't do that," in the exact tone she uses to lecture campers. Her need to exert discipline extends into her dreams, and all through the night she orders children to obey.

Fatigue catches up with me, and sometime before dawn I'm jolted by her hoarse command: "Get up." It's still dark, and I take a few seconds to reacquaint myself with my surroundings. Even this cot had seemed, finally, a sanctuary—at least from consciousness. I'd buried my head in a mildewed pillow and nuzzled myself into a damp dream that I was home.

No place could be as foreign as Ava's bungalow before dawn. There seems to be an actual fog inside, hanging in wisps between us, and the dank air is scarcely discernible from the chill outdoors.

Another follow-me crook of her fingers. She leads me out of the building, through a misted meadow, then down a narrow footpath. At the end of this trail rests a small lake, almost completely obscured in the haze. A doe, drinking, looks up and leaps away, white tail waving. I barely register this astonishing sight, when I turn to see Ava step out of her nightgown.

She stands naked, her skin hanging from her bones, a leather casing a size large on her angular frame. She has a brown, shriveled look, rather like the dried fruit she subsists on, as a practicing fruitarian. She raises both arms in the classic diver's pointed pose. I see her breasts—they have a sad, emptied look—sway. Then Ava arches her back and dives in, disappearing beneath the white fog. . . .

*A*va and I have awakened too early: Camp doesn't begin for hours. There is nothing to do in this interval. We walk in silence back to the bungalow, sit on our opposite cots, and regard one another until summoned by an amplified voice, blaring, without a hint of cheer: "Rise and shine, rise and shine . . . wake up all the Bluebells, rise and shine. . . ."

Then Ava and I start the day again, and walk to the cafeteria for breakfast. As we cross the patchy lawn, wet with dew, I plead my case with Ava: Oh, please let me stay in the bunkhouse with Susan. I will do anything, anything. No, I'm told, if I'm to sleep anywhere it will be with my age group, the eight-year-old Bluebells. As a last resort, I ask if I can stay with my uncle Gabe in an adult cabin, only to be told he will be on the next bus back to the city. (Oh, why don't I go with him?)

Susan. Susan. I spot her in a row of ten-year-old Dandelions, filing toward their table. I dash to her side, only to reach her at the moment her buddy, the plump blonde, takes the seat beside her. Susan makes the introductions, her almond eyes slanting even more than usual (deceit?). The blonde is Roberta Zolotow and she lives near us, I'm told, back in the city.

Roberta is wearing a sailor cap, which prompts my instant suspicion: Is she now The Sailor? (Later in the day, I chance to run past the bunkhouse and spy Roberta heaving herself over the window ledge. She has her leg caught over the sill, and is suspended, squealing. I give her a boost up, with an interlocking finger grip, and hear Susan's voice, thick with passionate petulance, inside: "Hurry, your ship is leaving in an hour.")

Nonetheless, I am still eager to stay at Susan's side. I am willing to abdicate and let Roberta serve as The Sailor. I never volunteered for that duty.

No sooner am I at Susan's breakfast table, trying to wedge myself onto the bench as crowded as the rush-hour subway back home, than I feel the heavy heat of the law at my back. Manny lifts me, yanking from my underarms, and carries me to another bunk table.

"You must sit with the Violets," he says, a group whose name I mishear, with psychic accuracy, as the Violents. Why? Why? There's no logic to this situation. The Violets are two years older than the Dandelions; they wear brassières under their tee-shirts. The Violets are camper-counselors and, as such, appear caught between identities, not knowing whether to exercise authority or obey. (In the end, they have authority only over me.)

The head camper-counselor wants to know if I have had a B.M.? If I knew what a B.M. was, I might have the sense to say "Yes." But I don't know, so two glasses of prune juice are set down before me. (An unnecessary precaution at Camp Ava, where it turns out most of the children have diarrhea and do nothing *but* have B.M.s. Although never listed on the Activities Board, the main activity at Camp Ava is being doubled-over in an outhouse, while the other children perform a conga dance of agony, waiting their turns.)

The moment no one is watching me, I boomerang to Susan's side. She takes me to see her bunkhouse: rows of cots, with folded blankets, a bulletin board with "cards from home" pinned to the cork. She lets me in on the obvious: Camp Ava is "a mistake." She would not have come here had she known. Known what? That the mail is censored, that the gift boxes of candy shipped by parents are seized and divided amongst the entire camp population. She lifts a mattress and shows me contraband potato chips. The punishment is incorporated into the crime: the chips are mashed, almost inedible. We lick the flecks from our fingertips, as we plot our resistance movement. Susan is waiting only for her parents to visit so that we can escape in the back seat of their car. Until then, we must keep our wits about us, as Susan warns "a lot of kids here have dirty minds. Terrible things can happen to you here, if you're not careful."

If Susan is frightened, I should be doubly so—she has a higher threshold. Meanwhile, Susan tells me her new friend, Roberta Zolotow, is "all right" and that there will be some benefit in the friendship for me, too. Mr. Zolotow is a shoe manufacturer and, through complicated arrangements with Manny and Ava, has arranged to sell us sandals at incredible discounts. (It is revealed later that Mr. Zolotow has gotten a kickback on the shoe business, and his daughter's camp tuition is "thrown in.")

That evening, Mr. Zolotow pulls up in a battered sedan and displays his wares with all the dispatch of a drug dealer. He whistles softly, and we tiptoe to the open trunk of his car, where he has sandal samples. (It turns out he is working yet another angle, in which he withholds some sandal surplus profit from Manny and Ava.) Mr. Zolotow is pink and plump, like his daughter, but he seems kindly enough as he sweats through his shirt, and talks "straps." I select a pink plastic model, and slip him a single dollar bill, my entire allowance, as a deposit. He vows to return in two weeks with the real sandals, in my size.

By the time Mr. Zolotow reappears, I'm past caring that he

has returned with an entirely different pair of shoes. Instead of the pink strappy number, he sells me a pair of mustard-colored moccasins. I don't understand how he could make such a mistake, but I give him the remainder of my life savings (six dollars), and run off in the "wrong" shoes.

I am living in flight of my bunkmates, the overage "Violents," who have sworn to strip me before the season is over. They have stripped each other, repeatedly, and I'm the only prey left. Hanging on to my weak-waisted underpants, I spend most of my time hiding.

The Violets are an older, more frightening version of my familiar friends, their games a heightened, rustic version of the old neighborhood scenarios. Each day they spend several hours lying in ambush outside the boys' latrine, hoping to see the boys pee. At night they play kissing games—Spin the Bottle, Blind Man, Mail Man. The older or more-developed girls play male roles, so that everyone can practice for the romances that lie directly up ahead. "We have to fake it. We need experience" is an oft-stated remark.

Not all the Violets need practice. One already has had experience. Toni Bloom, whose neck is already ringed with the purple "hickeys" of diverted lust, has done everything short of going all the way. After a date with a boy camper-counselor, Toni reports: "We were grinding all night."

I think of The Sailor and his permanent erection, and try to spy on the boy camper-counselor. Is he, as Susan predicted, now permanently afflicted? He appears to be. When he dances with girls in the Social Hall, they complain "it" jabs them in the thigh.

Yes, it must be permanent. "We keep grinding," Toni reports, after each session. Grinding. I imagine their sexual gears gnashing, caught in reverse. It doesn't sound pleasurable. But in our social group, while we seek experience, no one expects it to feel particularly pleasant. Sex is still something to be endured, eventually, so that we can have "kids like us." With Diana and Susan, I still wear a badge of honor: my mother had to submit only once, while their mothers had to suffer repeated acts to produce their sisters and brothers.

"I'm going all the way this summer," Toni predicts daily. "I'm not going home without experience." Meanwhile, she leads the strip raids in the communal shower. With a high cry, she seizes a wet naked girl each morning or evening, and tosses the victim onto the playing field. This was what I had seen on the afternoon of my arrival. That camper had been especially unfortunate, chosen for the ultimate humiliation—thrown on the field while boys marched past.

This girl, having reverted to thumb sucking, now hung back, last in her bunk line. There were other victims staggering around Ava. One, a retarded girl, whose face appeared sloped, as if reflected in a spoon, submitted to repeat strippings without protest, but was often spotted sitting on a bench staring into the air. Another girl, who wore clothes in the shower, was finally stripped in the morning sunlight, and thrown onto the field during reveille. "Look," cried Toni, "she has six tits."

Thereafter known as Sixtits, this pale girl did not speak, unless forced to, for the rest of the summer. When anyone new arrived, Sixtits was stripped again, so that they could see for themselves—the medical anomaly: she had six perfect pink nipples, in a double row down her chest. "Like a dog," Toni always said.

In this atmosphere, I become expert at dodging. I dart to the shower before anyone wakes, or rely on my daily dip in the pond to keep clean. I lie low in the bunkhouse, ever on guard. I sense my days are numbered and they are. . . .

Soon more vital problems take precedence. I have taken a secret vow not to eat any food that I have not eaten with my mother, and her menu is not featured at Camp Ava. So quite soon I am half-starved, living on the occasional banana or cookie.

This selectivity may temporarily work in my favor, for I escape the acute diarrhea that has most of the camp in an abdominal grip. During the long insomniac nights, I listen to the moaning from the toilets and see the silhouettes of the sufferers on line, in the moonlight outside. The camp food must be high in salmonella. Every day at lunch someone vomits on the floor of the cafeteria. With the unselective curiosity that younger children have, the littlest girls and boys circle the vomit puddle and analyze its molecular makeup: "It was the tuna salad." Sometimes, the attraction-repulsion is so strong a child retches in response, adding to the original pool.

Gift packages arrive from home, but these are always searched for contraband by Ava. Any box of candy must be evenly divided, so single M&M's are passed down the line. The children protest this—one M&M is worse than none: most candies have to be gulped by the fistful to be satisfying. "This is Communism," Susan explains.

Unknowingly, Ava drives her campers politically toward the right. If this is Communism, the Bluebells, the Violents, and the Dandelions are against it.

As the days turn to weeks, matters become life-threatening. I take to a feral existence, still sleeping in the Violents' bunk, but at all other times haunting the fringes of the camp, often near the garbage cans, like a raccoon (who also does this). The "Chef" takes pity on me, and when no one's looking, comes to the back door, and tosses me a cheese Danish.

By now, I also develop the digestive trouble that afflicts most of the campers, but I am too embarrassed to admit it. I have accidents but tell no one. Instead I become the Raskolnikov of lapsed toilet training, guiltily trying to hide the evidence. I seem always to be on some furtive mission connected to the cover-up: digging deeper holes to bury the underpants or checking the toilet to see if my attempt to flush away my underwear has succeeded (it hasn't).

Woozy and miserable, on the run from the Violents (who threaten "You're next"), I have only one goal left in life: to be allowed to stay in the same bunkhouse with Susan.

A bunk has "opened up." Susan shows it to me: the cot beside her own, with the sheets neatly tucked, a pillow stuffed at the headboard, a blanket folded at the foot. "Oh, God," I turn to prayer, "please, God, just let me sleep here . . ."

I lie down . . . to get the feel, and am spotted by Susan's counselor, who reports the illegal act to Manny. Manny looms above me and picks me up. He is carrying me out of the bunkhouse, when, for the first time, I decide to fight back. I kick, surprising myself as well as Manny when the toe of my Ked connects with the "gushy" bag between Manny's legs. He drops me fast and starts howling: "You little bastard . . ."

I'm off and running, round the bend of the driveway, past the Social Hall . . . through the chain-link gates and onto the real paved road. Down, down, my sneakers pound the asphalt: a steep descent. I hear Manny yell after me: "Look at that crazy kid, running away. Let her go."

And away I go. Fast with the exhilaration of escape. I will run to New York. I run for what seems to be a mile, all downhill, hurtling forward, the descent so pitched I feel I could topple over myself. Then the road snaking down the mountainside takes on an unfamiliar look. I see trees, boulder formations I don't remember. Is this the way we came here? How far is it to the Bronx?

A stitch in my side, and a pang in my heart. I pause, gasping, hide behind a tree at the roadside. At first the summer afternoon is perfectly still—I don't hear anyone in pursuit. Birds tweet, crickets chirp. Then I see the car, and it appears—slightly wavy in the humid air—rolling toward me in slow motion. Manny is at the wheel, calling with feigned concern: "Lily, Lily . . ."

Anger renews my strength and I take off into the woods. I tear through brambles, barely note I'm scratched in my haste. Counselors can now be heard, fanning out in the woods, calling, "Lily, Lily, there are bears. Lily, the bogeyman comes out at night. . . ."

I have no intention of surrender. I run deeper into the woods, toward a shadow that extends into a natural corridor. There I find a grove, as decorous as a lounge. Neatly skirted pine trees stand in a circle on a mauve carpet of soft needles. A large flat rock sits, a natural coffee table, in the center.

The stillness gives me pause. This is the enchanted forest I'd envisioned, the place Camp Ava was supposed to be. A silver brook flashes nearby, with a musical gurgle.

"I'll live here," I decide. With my knowledge of Indian skills,

I can build a small lean-to, subsist on berries. I find what I need—long, polelike branches—and lean them against a tree, then pack in matted leaves and twigs. Within an hour I have a partial shelter, and am sitting there, as deeper shadows fall, and the night song of insects begins. . . .

This is the time, I sense, to invoke the ultimate charm: I shut my eyes, draw up the force of my being, and beam it upward. I try a whispered call: "Rosie."

The answering silence is dense. Resistance, like the humidity, is in the air. She will come to me now; she has to. . . . I whisper louder, louder: "Rosie, Rosie . . ."

I count to ten, shut my eyes, and whisper her name again.

The silence remains: a profound reply. And then, for the first time, I truly know: she will never find me. I will never see Rosie again.

Now: shouts, running steps behind my lean-to: not my mother; Manny. I try to run again, but the breath is gone out of me. I stagger, feeling stabbed in my side, and stumble into what turns out to be a drainage ditch. I lie down there, my tears running into the mud, and above me Manny says, "Keep it up—you'll be sent to an orphanage."

He slings me over his shoulder, and carries me to the car. I sit in the back, as his prisoner, and am driven into the camp.

Later that night, I scribble a postcard plea to my uncles, an appeal so desperate it reads: "Come get me yesterday."

By the time my uncles arrive, the situation has, as they say in wartime, escalated. I am camped out on the basketball court, next to Susan's bunkhouse. I will never go back to the Violents, I swear. I will stay here, on this buckling asphalt, until they let me have the empty cot alongside Susan.

The moon rises, dew forms, but I will not give in. I will sleep on the court rather than return to the older girls' bunkhouse. What I can't tell Manny or Ava: that afternoon, after two weeks of living in fear of just such an attack, I have been stripped.

The Violents, led by Toni Bloom, caught me off guard in a near-semiconscious state—I had slipped into a deserted cabin to be alone, and had fallen into a reverie. I had slid down onto the floor, my back against the screen door, and let my mind wander. A warm sun had streamed upon me, lulling me deeper into the trance. I was living in the forest, with warriors who had pinto ponies and a birch-bark canoe, when the Violents burst in, more savage than the enemy tribe in my other life. They rammed the door so that I fell forward, onto my face, and one girl grabbed one leg, and another the other leg. They had my shorts off in seconds, and the underpants. I twisted and kicked, anything to keep my legs together, but they pried them apart.

"She has no hairs," someone said.

And then they were gone, leaving me on the wood floor, too stunned to cry. Oddly enough, perhaps because so many painful events have preceded this one, I am not as devastated as I would have expected. (Maybe I was too destroyed to suffer any more damage.) I discover I have my own strength—it comes from being already broken.

That's it. I'm not going to be pushed around anymore. I march off to Susan's bunkhouse and announce my intention. There is soon a major confrontation on the basketball court. My uncles have been called and summoned from the city. Manny, Ava, and a half-dozen other counselors circle me, but don't dare touch. Maybe I finally have the right glare in my eyes.

"She'll give in," Ava says. "Let her sit here until she freezes her tushy off."

At this point in the deadlock, Uncles Len and Gabe arrive by taxi. Their arrival is not undramatic on its own terms: Uncle Gabe, always a victim of motion sickness, staggers from the cab, retching and reeling. He has a temperature, and a refugee doctor is called. Uncle Gabe is led off to the camp infirmary.

Which leaves Uncle Len to deal with the situation on the basketball court. The moon backlights Len as he stalks toward us. . . . A giant figure, costumed as usual in trenchcoat and fedora, and walking heavily in size 13 shoes. His shadow looms across the lawn. In reality, he is six feet six. In this light, he appears at least nine feet tall.

He carries a leather portfolio and a manila envelope: he enters the arena as if approaching the bench in Civil Court. His soft voice is weighted with even more emphasis than usual, and he speaks formally, as always, of "an altercation" and the "possibility of negotiation."

The basic dispute is outlined for him. I have to stay with Susan, I say. The Manny-Ava team tell him I must stay in my assigned bunk. If they break the rules for me, all the other campers will "want the same thing."

Uncle Len leads Manny and Ava a short distance from where I sit, cross-legged, in center court. They confer under the hoop. "I must remonstrate with you," he says. "We are talking about a child who lost her mother a few weeks ago. She needs to be with the friend who is most familiar to her. Can't you make an exception in this case?"

No. They can't. Voices are raised. In the Dandelion bunk, faces, including Susan's, appear framed in the windows.

Len says he must caution Manny and Ava. He doesn't like raised voices. His own voice remains grave, low, in his usual presidential style: "We are gathered here tonight on this field . . ."

Uncle Len makes a few attempts at détente. He offers his favorite solution to any problem—call another cab and check into a hotel. Then everyone can reconsider the situation in the morning.

I lie down on the asphalt. No, I'm not moving. A young boy counselor unexpectedly rushes forward, pleading: "Do it for me. I taught you to swim and dive."

It's a ploy. "I knew how to swim and dive before I met you."

Ava says I can hold office in the Violents bunk. I can be a vice president, if I go back.

No. I'm bitter and insulted by their change in tactics, now that my uncle is here. I say: "Don't use child psychology on me." Only I can't pronounce "psychology."

Uncle Len tries to reason with Manny and Ava: "Come on, you're adults. This is a little girl. Let her go in there."

Manny and Ava announce a stalemate. They are retiring to their own bungalows. Len calls out after them that "this action is ill-advised" and will have serious "repercussions."

I don't know what "repercussions" are, but I like the sound of them. And I'm not budging, although it is getting colder, and I start to shiver. Uncle Len takes off his trenchcoat and covers me. Then, to my surprise, he lies down on the court, too. "They're a tough bunch," he confides, "but we can prevail." Like a boxing fan after watching a good match, Len compliments "my spirit." Reliving the exchanges, Len quotes my retorts, and, for the first time, we laugh together.

As the moon and stars brighten in the night sky, our talk turns otherworldly. Len points out the constellations, and we discuss eternity, immortality, our place in this universe. This is my first real look at all the stars; back home, the city light bleached out the heavens. At night, even when my mother and I stood on the rooftop of AnaMor Towers, all we could see was Venus and the violet glow cast by the twi-night doubleheaders.

Seeing the big picture opens up more possibilities. For the first time, I ask if it's possible that when people die they don't really die, but go to live on other planets? Is it possible that parallel planets exist, where our missing people live out their lives "exactly the same?" I am imagining my mother on Mars, with a duplicate daughter.

Uncle Len sounds faintly dubious, but doesn't dismiss this theory: "It's possible." Len and I explore more possibilities for an afterlife. We share a certain skepticism regarding heaven. I have to ask, if there is such a place, doesn't it get overcrowded? And what would someone like Manny or Mrs. Hassan do there? It's hard to picture them yelling and cleaning in heaven.

"They're concerned with trivia," Uncle Len agrees (this turns out to be his favorite assessment of people he "deals with" on the "petty" problems they "invent"). We decide that if there is an afterlife it's not for everyone, just for some. Only a few people have souls. Lives concerned only with "material things" (another Len expression) end, but if people live for ideas and feelings, they may exist forever.

I want to know why so many people are cruel. "There's no why," answers Uncle Len. Most people "on the outside" don't care, and their indifference seems to be a kind of cruelty. They can behave badly or simply vanish. "Most things happen without reason," Len sums up. "Life is often a motiveless crime."

I am pondering this concept, so different from the "God-will-punish-you" ethic of AnaMor Towers and Camp Ava, when Manny, in bathrobe and slippers, comes flapping back to the court. Uncle Len rises, reaching eye level with the hoop and towering over the squat Manny. Manny seems to diminish in defeat, growing shorter by the second. Uncle Len says in his softest, but somehow most threatening tone: "I'm taking Lily in there now."

Manny scrunches his face into submission, but is still ungracious. "Do what you want. We don't need a lawsuit if you catch pneumonia out here."

"That's very wise," says Len, escorting me to the plank steps of Dandelion House. We open the door. The ten-year-old girls are stretched out in a long gray line of lumped forms. I take my place among them, and prepare for my first real rest since my mother's death. In her sleep Susan smacks her lips, seemingly in approval. I climb onto "my" bed, and, before settling down, peek out the window:

Uncle Len, waving his fedora, is walking backward across the court.

$\mathcal{T}$he basketball-court victory is the high point of my torture vacation. I stagger onward, committed to the season, and staying with Susan.

I'm not the only one hurting: Uncle Gabe is sweating it out in the camp infirmary, where he is the only adult. He stays for almost the entire season, the victim of a mystery illness, and, it turns out, improper medical care.

The refugee doctor is now exposed as a refugee dentist: "He couldn't find work here, so he made up the part with the medical degree." Ava and Manny are surprisingly tolerant of this disclosure, and the dentist-doctor is allowed to practice ("He comes when we need him" is the Ava bottom line). He has also given Uncle Gabe a massive overdose of antibiotics to wipe out what began as a routine flulike infection.

"'Antibiotic' is right," reports Uncle Gabe from his bed when I visit. "It's killed off everything in my body. The huge dosage killed off not just the bad bacteria but the good bacteria." Although, ascetic that he is, Uncle Gabe can't keep a touch of pride from creeping into his complaint: "There are no germs of any type in my body."

It turns out you need the good germs to stay healthy, which leaves Uncle Gabe in the camp infirmary in "a weakened condition." His condition remains mysterious (and stays with him for the next decade). I'm never told exactly what is wrong with Gabe, but his condition is always referred to in terms of fire: "It's flaring up again." He is treated with aluminum-foil suppositories, which I dub his "silver bullets."

In spite of flare-ups, Uncle Gabe finds solace at Camp Ava. He claims to be inspired by the proximity to "nature." When he totters onto the denuded "lawn," he seems not to notice that there is more actual grass growing on the asphalt basketball court. He cuts a strange figure, in maroon cotton pajamas, exploring the Ava boundaries, picking ragweed, although it aggravates his "sinus."

"No one ever promised me it was easy to be a pioneer," Gabe says. Even in his shaky health, he finds the strength to enter the Camp Ava Talent Competition. On stage in the Social Hall, the lights glancing off his eyeglasses, Gabe belts out his original Jewish gospel hit:

"How did Moses ever know / Over ten thousand years ago . . . / About love and charity, / Clean living with so much clarity? / Oh, how did Moses ever know?"

He wins second prize: a pressure cooker.

He takes to the camp in the spirit of Hans Castorp in *The Magic Mountain:* evenly dividing his time between daily hikes to promote health and sessions of suffering.

I often take the daily nature hike with Gabe, and teach him the few country songs I know. . . . He sings full-out, charging on through the woods, and I run to keep up with him. One afternoon he gets a headstart, and I see him loping along a mountain trail, his hat tilting precariously backward, as he moves toward the sunset, singing: "Oh my darling, oh my darling, / Oh my darling Clementine, / You are lost but not forgotten, / Oh my Darling Clementine. . . ."

I teach him my favorite tune, "Red River Valley," and later, from his infirmary bed, he croons: "Oh, they say you are leaving this valley. . . ."

My uncles leave Camp Ava, assuring me that they are returning to the city to set up "our new home." They would take me
with them, but by then I'm resigned to my fate (what else can
happen to me?).

I endure the remaining weeks by escaping into the camp's
single interesting geological feature: an Indian cave. While the
other campers commit crimes or participate in activities, I hide
out in the cave, where I am soon joined by a twelve-year-old boy,
Frankie, who for unknown reasons has also failed to fit in at
Camp Ava.

The cave is the sanctuary I have sought. A counselor confides
that it was once occupied by Mohawk Indians, and that Ava discovered the place and found a pile of ancient beads, which turned
to powder at her touch.

Frankie, a handsome boy with bright, believing eyes and long
legs, is more than willing to enact my Indian scenarios. We come
close to the scenes I have always imagined at bedtime: I nurse the
wounded warrior back to health. Both Frankie and I are covered
with cuts and bruises, and we spend hours attending to our scabs,
giving them clinical care and charting every color change.

I immediately fall in love with Frankie, and he wants to spend
all his free time with me. "You're not like the other girls," he says.

We never kiss or touch—other than to peel off damaged
skin—but, sure enough, Frankie is soon accused of wrongdoing.
Ava banishes him to the outskirts of camp; he is not allowed to
play with me.

From then on, I count the days—the season seems to last cen-
turies. Finally: escape. Susan's parents drive up, a week before the
official end. The Hassans offer to give me a lift back to town, if I

promise, on all I hold sacred, to eat rare roast beef on the ride home.

I raise my hand and swear "I will." Secretly I know I won't— I never eat rare meat, and I am still keeping my dietary vows not to eat foods I didn't eat "before." There follows a fight at a roadhouse rest stop, which ends with Mrs. Hassan trying to force bloody beef into my mouth. We ride the rest of the way home in silence. Mr. Hassan sneaks me an occasional Lifesaver when his wife isn't looking. When he winks at me, in the rear-view mirror, Mr. Hassan reminds me, with his dark eyes, of Uncle Len.

*H*omecoming: Uncle Len is there, pacing the street in front of AnaMor Towers, anxious not to miss the moment of my arrival. He holds a bakery box with a welcome-home blueberry pie.

Surely I have never been so glad to see anyone in my life. And upstairs, on the other side of AnaMor Towers, is 7G, our new apartment, a junior four.

The apartment hierarchy in AnaMor Towers starts with "efficiency" apartments (the smallest, cheapest), moves up a grade to "deluxe one bedroom," and then peaks with a "junior four," an apartment that features one large bedroom and one "junior" bedroom, a nook off the kitchen, where it is assumed a child will sleep.

With a child's smugness, I don't question their choice. Of course they want to stay with me. It doesn't occur to me that Uncle Len and Uncle Gabe are the least likely candidates to become my guardians.

I do not consider what upheaval this may cause in their personal and professional lives. In fact, they are making an acute adjustment to what Len calls "the situation."

They had been living similar but separate existences in different boroughs—Len in Manhattan, Gabe in Brooklyn. The move brought them under the same roof for the first time since their own youth.

(Years later, I wonder why they moved in with me, and not the other way around. My home was inconveniently situated, offering them nothing but the dull routine of two-hour round-trip subway rides to their respective jobs. Yet they came to me. And, knowing them, I can guess why. They chose to disrupt their own lives to avoid further destroying mine. I would be allowed to remain in the same building, attend the same school, keep the same friends.)

Eavesdropping that first night, I overhear Len tell Gabe: "We don't want her to be insecure." I wonder: what does "insecure" mean?

During our early days together, I busy myself with the domestic arrangements. In our new apartment, we create a home never envisioned in the architect's rendering of a junior four. We establish a household where eccentricity is the norm. Uncle Len does not believe in furniture, so he provides what he calls "alternatives."

"People get bogged down by possessions," Len explains. "Then the possessions own them." He also dislikes crowding. He loves to see the dimensions of a room, unobstructed by such things as armchairs, couches, and coffee tables.

He has always lived in furnished hotel apartments, and prides himself on traveling light. He moves in with two manila envelopes, a portrait of Lincoln, and four file cabinets. Len favors the file cabinets over ordinary bureaus. He shows me how to "file" my clothes, alphabetically.

We are also filed—choosing our areas in the apartment. I trot straight to the sunlit large bedroom at the back. Having never had a room of my own, I have instant dreams of grandeur.

"No," Uncle Gabe demurs, "that room is too big for a little girl." He points to the tiny junior room, off the kitchen, which is, as Uncle Len later points out, "smaller than a regulation prison cell."

Uncle Len, already a fool for love, sets down the beer he has been drinking on the floor of the tiny room: "Where I set down this bottle, that's where I sleep."

Uncle Gabe shakes his head. "If that's what you want, Shaine, but I think you're spoiling her."

In fact, they both spoil me, by giving me a free hand in all matters of décor. The result is interior decoration that looks exactly like what it is—an apartment designed by an eight-year-old.

When the house painters arrive, with chips and charts, I choose the color scheme: orange, pink, and white.

"She knows what she wants," says Uncle Gabe, impressed as I direct the decoration of 7G. I instruct the painters to paint the walls in different colors, and, when they decline to paint candy stripes, I finish that job myself. Our dinette area is duly striped in honor of my favorite ice-cream pop, the orange-vanilla Humorette.

"Very stylish," my uncles agree.

Uncle Len adds a few touches of his own, in deference to my femininity. He paints everything else that can be painted—pink. Including the television set. When he installs my file cabinet, he gives that a coat of pink, too. Len's painting style is determined by how much extra paint remains in a bucket: he keeps painting as long as the supply lasts. He paints utilitarian items that don't usually get paint jobs: radios, toasters, wastebaskets.

We travel, *en masse,* by bus to make "emergency expenditures." We buy beds and (against Len's wishes) a couch.

As a family, we stand out among the shoppers at Bedland. I run up and down aisles of mattresses, and intermittently jump on them. If one feels right, I curl into a fetal position.

The sales clerks can't believe my uncles let me do this. Len and Gabe show me serious respect. "How does it feel, Lily? Is that the one?"

I choose: a little-girl-sized twin bed for myself (my first real bed, not a cot) and a giant bed for Uncle Len, which we all immediately call "the aircraft carrier."

Gabe and I discuss the issue of couch *versus* studio bed for himself. Although Len campaigns against "a big ugly piece of furniture," Gabe and I announce we have plans to entertain and, because Gabe will be sleeping in the living room, a convertible couch will be the most attractive, socially acceptable choice.

With Uncle Len wagging his massive head—no, no—we all go to Castro Convertibles, where I leap from couch to couch, yanking each sofa open in turn. We choose, as always, from "emergency" goods: floor models that are ready for immediate delivery.

Tossing foam seat cushions in the air, I make my selection, based on ease of converting and color: a massive sofa, covered in gold lamé.

"Very glamorous" is Uncle Gabe's assessment, although already he is concerned about his back.

Uncle Len agrees, "under duress" as he puts it, to buy the couch, but he holds the line against armchairs. "In Japan, people have no furniture," he keeps saying, as we tour dinette sets. "They sit on mats. Everything rolls up, and can be stored."

(This turns out to be a key to Len's approach to life. He doesn't like possessions, but he *does* like gadgets that can be folded for storage, or that have historical significance. Very soon he turns up with a collapsible "camouflage" bike. "Used for the invasion of Normandy," he explains. "The bikes folded so that our guys could jump out of planes holding them. When they landed, they could pedal away from the Germans.")

Gabe and I apply pressure to force Len to agree to a dinette set: "Oh, God, this will bog us down." He wants us to eat on the floor, picnic-style. I'm interested, but Gabe refuses. He wants to "entertain" and has visions of dinner parties.

Again I choose: hot-salmon-colored chairs, surrounding a black-white-and-pink Formica table, with enough trim for a Cadillac bumper. "Very stylish," Gabe approves.

Once launched as interior decorator, I am quickly out of control. Although I disdain Mrs. Hassan, I have secretly coveted her wall-to-wall carpeting for years, and now start a campaign to cover our new floors in off-white plush.

The uncles draw the line there, with Len extolling the virtues of gleaming wood, and Gabe agreeing that for ease in cleaning, wood might be best. As a compromise gesture, they buy me a pink bathmat.

As soon as we set up housekeeping, Len and Gabe institute elaborate schedules. I spend entire evenings instructing them on how "we" do things. I tell them how to prepare my favorite foods: tuna croquettes, burned hamburgers ("well-done" means gray inside, black outside), boiled hot dogs, and baked potatoes. Both Len and Gabe learn how to cook these foods but neither makes any distinction as to the hour that these items should appear on the menu—so tuna croquettes and hamburgers can and do appear at breakfast.

Within days, they decide on a division of labor based on individual talent and preference: Len cooks and Gabe cleans.

As hard as they both work, neither has a clue as to how these tasks are usually done, and the result is off-beat. Len's cooking is savory, but adheres to no known timetable. He also applies his logic to foods: "Why not popcorn for breakfast? People eat corn flakes, corn bread. . . . In the South, they eat corn fritters. Why not popcorn? Corn is corn."

Len also wears an "official" uniform in his capacity as chef: either a high chef's hat, or (on hot days) a pith helmet. (It's as hot in the kitchen as it is in the jungle or on the desert, so a pith helmet makes sense.) He has a professional apron, which he wears over his usual cooking outfit: tee-shirt and suit pants.

Soon known as "The King of the Pressure Cooker," Len masters complicated fricassees, but will also add a performance value to his cooking: "Watch the dancing lady on the pressure cooker." Once embarked on his culinary career, Len takes his responsibilities very seriously. He always has something "working" on the stove, and prides himself as cooking with few utensils and overcoming technical difficulties. When our new stove turns out to be dysfunctional, with only half the burners operative, Uncle Len declares himself up to the task: "Call me 'Two-Burner Len.'"

Meanwhile, Uncle Gabe cleans with a vengeance. He has a religious zeal against dirt. He is almost violent in his mop-and-pail-swinging attacks on grime. Innocent of the standard methods of home maintenance, Uncle Gabe buys name-brand cleansers but doesn't know their traditional functions. The result: he uses bathroom scouring powder on the wooden floors, and pours Clorox bleach on the polished parquet. After a few treatments, our new apartment floor seems to list, following in a physical way the social warp of our lives.

Our clothes, too, soon reflect the warp. Neither uncle has any solution to the laundry problem other than to ship it out to a commercial firm. This company, Consolidated Laundry, consolidates the creases. We send out sacks of soiled clothes and get back bags of shirts and blouses, immaculate but compressed. Their process seems to seal in the wrinkles, and we all wear fiercely creased clothes. Some of my dresses are so compressed that they appear inches shorter than their actual length. There has also been no attempt at color sorting, and a red blouse has stained our entire washable wardrobe. We have no choice but to fly family colors—everything we wear is dyed shades of pink.

My uncles' homemaking skills don't go unnoticed at Ana-

Mor Towers. While there are housewives who nod approval at my uncles, as they bustle in and out of the building with great sacks of cleansers and groceries, there are also the naysayers.

"What do two men know about keeping house and raising a child?" asks Mrs. Hassan, before she answers her own question: "Nothing."

*W*e come to regard "the outside" as not entirely friendly to our new household. Mrs. Hassan continually beats the drums for our home to fail: "They can't last, they can't last. . . ." And every time she sees me running past, she announces loudly, "That child should be taken out of that home."

Certainly, when we venture forth as a threesome, we must present an odd sight. When I return to school, my uncles escort me to the yard, where the children are sorted by grade and lined up by height. All the other children are accompanied by their mothers, or an occasional stray daddy. Only I arrive flanked by "Unkies."

"The Unkies" (as I call them) appear on Open School Day also—looming at the rear of the classroom. Uncle Len, in slouch hat, shades, and trenchcoat, hunched over in the low-ceilinged room, looks particularly out of place. Uncle Gabe, accustomed to being around groups of small children, seems more at ease chatting with "the mothers."

I overhear Gabe confide to a woman that "Lily won't eat anything green."

Len's style, once he warms to the situation, is not to concentrate on problems but to praise me extravagantly. Presenting himself as a cross between Sam Spade and President Lincoln, Uncle Len wants to impress my teacher with what an exceptional child I am. "This isn't an ordinary little girl."

Dressed in my Indian-maiden costume (worn now on an almost daily basis), my waist-long hair tangled and incorrectly braided, wearing a Davy Crockett hat even on warm days . . . this is certainly true, but not in the way Uncle Len means. I am quite aware, now, that I am different. Two boys in my class have actually chased me across the yard, demanding to know the answers to two questions: Is it true my mother died? And do I really have a picture of a naked lady in my wallet?

I have no idea how the naked-lady rumor started, but my denials are ignored, my wallet peeled open and flung to the pavement. I realize, leaning in shock against the fence, that now an atmosphere of tragedy and scandal surrounds me.

In self-defense, I develop an eye for the irregularities in other children's lives. I spend my days in class studying the other students instead of the subjects. I watch with special interest those "kids" who seem to lead lives more peculiar than my own.

In my fourth-grade class, there are at least three children that merit my all-day attention: First and most haunting is the new girl, an ocher-colored girl, with a high frizz of ocher-colored hair that cannot be combed down, although her mother attempts to pin giant bows and barrettes on what is basically an Afro. Unofficial but obvious is the fact that this little girl, also named Diana (I think of her as the ocher-colored Diana), must have a mixed-race parentage. It is whispered that her mother, a pale blonde, mated with a Negro.

Whoever her father is, the ocher-colored Diana never alludes to him, and he never appears on Open School Days. She lives across the street, and I see her go in and out of her building, always alone or with her mother. An aura of isolation is almost visible around her—brought on more by her sad expression, I believe, than her mixed parentage. She never speaks unless called on, and never plays on the street.

One afternoon she walks home, not beside but slightly behind me. When we near her house, she whispers, "Do you want to see?"

I follow her into a dark brick apartment building where a Norse Valkyrie cast in cement guards the door. The ocher-colored Diana lives in a fiercer architectural fantasy than I do at AnaMor. These stone-faced women carry spears, and wear furs bearing fanged animal faces.

We climb the tiled stair slowly. I have a sense of ceremony in accompanying the ocher-colored girl home. Silent as ever, she takes a key from her dog-tag chains and unlocks her apartment door.

"It's in here," she says, taking me through an inner corridor. We pass her bed, oddly situated in the hall itself, so that we have to squeeze past to reach the apartment's single bedroom. "There is only one bed in here," she announces. "You know what that means."

I didn't, but I nod.

"Divorce."

She walks around the single bed, and points to the low head-board—and above that a round stain on the wall, where it appears someone using a hair oil has rested his head. The ocher-colored Diana traces the circle with her finger, and says: "My father left this."

As part of the ceremony, I too trace the outline of her father's grease spot, and again I nod, at the solemnity of the revelation. I *am* impressed, and I know why she has chosen me to view the sa-cred grease spot. I am the only child in the neighborhood who will look at that stain and feel . . . envy.

I watch the other different ones in class: there is a boy named Steven who is said to have suffered an injury to "his privates." He has lost some crucial part of himself in a fall from a barbed-wire fence. Now, on the edge of puberty, his voice is still climbing. He speaks in a mouse voice, squeaking his answers in class, and his hips seem to grow wider while we watch.

There are several girls with physical handicaps, but the one who mesmerizes me is Linda, who was born without a right arm, and wears what we call "a doll arm," a pink plastic prosthetic de-vice. Linda has the spirit that often seems to accompany affliction: she chooses to flaunt her doll arm, instead of hide it. She volun-teers to be a crossing guard, and it is she, waving her pink plastic mechanical hand, who ushers us daily into the schoolyard.

Here and there, in other classes, I spot more irregulars: the Krescott twins, John and Alan, who weighed eight pounds (jointly) at birth, and are still miniatures, dressed alike in hounds-tooth suits. They have a protective mother, who hovers at the fence and is known to pay them a dollar for every pound of weight they gain.

There is another girl, with a halo of frizzed golden hair, whose name is Guinevere. Guinevere appears never to bathe—her skin and her nylon blouse are the same tattle-tale gray. She doesn't talk to the other kids, but speaks constantly in a soft mumble into her own collarbone. Sometimes, if I am near her, I hear snatches of poetry. I imagine she comes from a very well-educated if not sanitation-minded home, for she seems to whisper Shakespearean sonnets under her breath. She is said to have a brother named Galahad.

Sometimes I divert my attention from the different ones to study the normal ones, who greatly outnumber the others. The girls have shining ponytails, wear coordinated outfits. The boys display neatly parted hair, and wear "sharp" sweaters. Well-groomed, slated for piano lessons, these children also exert a certain attraction. I usually develop a crush on the most blandly attractive boy: the one with the neatest hair, best-pressed clothes. I tend toward the very blond boys, like Frank Tuchek, but every once in a while I veer toward someone more swarthy. Paul, a new boy imported from Switzerland, soon becomes the Charles Boyer of the fourth grade. His difference is somehow more attractive than that of the other new boy, Fritz, who is from Rumania and is rumored to eat worms.

Why this sudden awareness of who is different and who isn't? My circumstances are making me conservative—at least at school. My days of whooping and hollering in the schoolyard seem in the past. I attend class, and doodle. Whatever it takes to lead escapes over the fence, I have—at least temporarily—lost it.

Sometimes I feel an aftershiver—a vibration that recalls the week of "sitting shiver." And I can't help but recall the years gone by, when it was Rosie who walked me to the first day of school.

Most of the time, though, I walk what Uncle Gabe calls "an even keel." ("But don't keel over," he adds.) However, when I write compositions, my pencil pauses at the date. Unless I concentrate, I automatically write the day my mother died. Something inside me has stopped telling time. If I wander away from school at lunchtime, I often forget to return. I don't do this intentionally—I simply lose track. One afternoon I run back to the school after what seems like an hour's lunch period only to find everyone else leaving—it's dismissal.

Three hours unaccounted for . . .

Often, inside, I feel this gutside of unease. Too much has changed. . . . It doesn't help to hear, one afternoon, that the little ocher-colored girl has been sent to a foster home.

"The mother was mental," reports Mrs. Hassan. "The child was taken from that home."

While "the outside" gives me a scaredy feeling, the inside of our new home becomes increasingly cozy. My uncles perform Herculean feats. Uncle Len commutes twice a day from his job in lower Manhattan, to be there when I come home for lunch.

"I was on an assignment in the neighborhood" is all he will say, but even at eight years old I know the arithmetic to a two-hour-round-trip subway ride twice a day—four hours in transit to make a peanut-butter-and-jelly sandwich. Uncle Gabe takes "the afternoon shift," as they refer to it. He rushes home to be there when school lets out. He runs from the subway stop, and I usually greet him halfway. We meet on the street near the statuette of Babe Ruth and exchange a chocolate bar (his) and kisses (mine).

Inside our apartment, we are gradually creating customs and inventing our own special language. In many ways the life we live inside our candy-striped orange-pink-and-white apartment is as different from a conventional family's as it appears. Without the possibility of assigning roles by gender, my uncles play mother and father, interchangeably.

There is a continuous exchange of information. While they are learning how to raise a little girl (with direct instructions from the one involved), that little girl is learning how to manage two unmarried men in their mid-years. In the process, three disparate (some might even say mismatched) individuals become a family.

We observe a strict etiquette in matters concerned with gender. At the very start, when it's time for me to take my bath, Uncle Gabe tells his brother: "Let me handle this—I have the know-how. . . ." He reaches for the phone to call the same aunt he'd phoned during my pre-camp days with him.

"I can take a bath myself," I announce, and do so, while both uncles wait in suspense on the other side of the bathroom door. I

send a two-inch flood cascading across the floor, but after an en-
ergetic mop-up by the uncles the event is declared a qualified success.

We always refer to bath time as "performing ablutions." As in
"Will you be performing your ablutions this evening?"

Uncle Len keeps a razor and a mirror hanging in the shower,
so he can perform all his ablutions in one hectic lather.

Gabe's style in this area is antiquated far beyond his age (he is
only thirty-eight). He still shaves with a straight-edge razor and
brush, uses tooth powder instead of toothpaste, and refers to any
undergarments left in the bathroom as "unmentionables."

A certain formality of speech may run in the family, as Uncle
Len always uses an elaborate form of address in lieu of colloqui-
alisms. In the morning, instead of pounding on my door to yell,
"Time to get up for school" (as happens in most homes, I imag-
ine), Uncle Len will tap lightly and whisper, "Lily . . . Lily . . .
D." (the initial stands for my new nickname, "Doll"). . . . "Lily
D., the Board of Education would like to see you today. . . . The
Board of Education requests your presence. . . ."

Uncle Len adds other linguistic flourishes. Perhaps as carry-
over from his mysterious travels, he often adds foreign accents to
ordinary nouns. Particularly, he spices up mealtimes by adding
"el" as in "Would you care for el omeletto?" He also adds Spanish syllables to refer to people he doesn't like. Our landlord, Morris Snezak, is only referred to around our house as "El Creepo."
And any evil person is known here as "El Beasto."

Other romance-language touches are added to jazz up what
could otherwise sound prosaic. Instead of "Will you be home tonight?" Len might ask Gabe: "Can you hold down the hacienda?"

Our junior four is never called "the apartment" —only "the fort," "the ranch," or "the hacienda." So it makes sense that, when we retire for the evening, we say goodnight in pseudo-Spanish: "Buenos noches" becomes "Good noche." Then "Good noche" quickly degenerates further into "Good nouchy." Finally our official sign-off round at bedtime is: "Good nouchy, wake up grouchy."

Uncle Len also adds an investigative influence. No one notices exactly when we start to do this, but early on in our living together the proper response to "Who's there?" on the other side of the door is "It is I, another suspect."

Anyone left alone in the hacienda is said to be "on their own recognizance."

The uncles also use legal jargon to settle any family arguments. Uncle Len is the undisputed head of our judicial system. He presides, Solomon-like, over all important decisions.

For minor matters, we go to his Small Claims Court. A test case—

Gabe and I start out in Small Claims Court (Uncle Gabe doesn't want me to drink so much soda). The case moves to Civil Court—

Me: "But you promised me I could have two bottles a week."

Gabe: "But you didn't drink the two bottles; you saved up until you had six bottles, and then drank them all at once."

On to the Supreme Court: "Wasn't that my right?"

Uncle Len rules in my favor: I have the right to hoard cream soda, and binge at the end of the month, if I want to.

Uncle Gabe abides by the ruling, although he protests the result is not in the spirit of the law.

Uncle Len wields a spice mallet, which he pounds on the Formica podium. "Justice has been served."

Court adjourned.

I have my own language, too, mostly based on malapropisms and mispronunciations. My uncles enjoy my mistakes so much we usually incorporate them into our foreign tongue.

One night when my uncles become hopelessly entangled in a discussion of household chores, I reprimand them, asking, "What is all this non-ess?" meaning "nonsense." From then on, it's always "noness" in our house. I have an entire vocabulary of similar mispronunciations. "Deny" somehow comes out "denny" as in "Don't denny it," and a number of these expressions find their way into permanent usage.

I also make incorrect assumptions. Because both uncles have hernia belts that they sling over the bathtub towel rack at night, I imagine this is standard male equipment. In fact, I think a hernia is another sex organ, an unseen one, restrained by the belt.

No one sets me straight on that one for years.

There is especially delicate etiquette determining the uncles' romantic lives.

When Uncle Len announces a "secret mission" on a Saturday night, I know he has a date. In fact, he has a steady girlfriend, a great-breasted brunette named Frederica. He has stacks of onion-skin love letters, written in fine violet script, hidden (he thinks) in his closet. I have, of course, read them, and so know that he has been passionately involved with Frederica for over ten years.

It's clear from her letters that Frederica would like to marry Uncle Len. But Uncle Len has been lightly ducking out of matrimony for more years than anyone, including Gabe, can recall. On any social occasion, Len has a way of disappearing into the background—or even darting out the door. At family weddings, he stands as far to the rear as possible, wearing one of his many disguises. He loves to go out "incognito" and has a way of seeming elusive even when present.

I watch other relatives corner Len and ask, "When will we see you again?" only to receive one of his ambiguous replies: "In due course." He lives with me, but curious cousins will hear only: "I maintain several addresses."

I'm sure that he has perfected this secretive style in the romance arena. He is a man with an unlisted number—for whom the phone rings.

Len occasionally takes me along on a liaison. Whenever I see Frederica, she tells me how much she loves Len, and how nice it would be to marry him. "Marriage is not a probability" is all Len will ever say on the subject. I have a hunch that her apartment, if dusted for his fingerprints, would come up "blind."

Romantically, Uncle Gabe is an opposite number. He courts women and dreams of marriage. He constantly squires women on his standard version of a date: first, a hansom-cab ride through Central Park, then dinner and a show. After which, on the long rides to see them home (he often, for some reason, dates women from as far away as Staten Island, affording Gabe several hours to, as he would put it, "plead his troth"), he wraps up every evening by singing one of his own love songs, and dedicating it in the lady's honor.

Len and I are not too surprised that these tactics don't work. Uncle Gabe also has a dream of converting nonreligious women to his deep orthodox faith. Uncle Len doesn't encourage him in this plan, and I hear him use the word "unrealistic" to describe Gabe's entire courting style.

The uncles trade off Saturday nights: one weekend one will go out, while the other "holds down the fort." But all nights end with the inevitable exchanges:

"Good nouchy . . ."

"Wake up grouchy."

"Good nouchy."

"Wake up grouchy."

After a particularly lively Saturday night, someone might add a cheery "Yedda-bravo!", a cry whose origin no one can remember.

*A*s soon as we settle in, Uncle Gabe begins a campaign to bring me into his religion. He works so hard to convert me that I am reluctant to confide that I am already a practicing pagan. While he is urging me to attend Sabbath services at Young Israel, I secretly worship at an altar to the "Great Spirit" in my closet.

As if my Native American faith (I constantly seek my manitou in the park) isn't sacrilegious enough, I am also experimenting with a new religion at school. There I have the good fortune to be blessed with a beautiful and reverent teacher, Miss Eisen, who is busily winning her fourth graders over to the gods of Ancient Greece.

This lovely young lady (she is twenty-four years old) spends an hour a day reading aloud from Hamilton's *Mythology.* I am transported . . . instantly. It's not a gigantic leap from AnaMor Towers to Mount Olympus. Miss Eisen, sensing my interest, invites me to work on a special tribute to the gods. She appoints me art monitor and I meet her at 7:30 a.m. every school day to paint a life-size mural of Phaeton driving his chariot into the sun.

"Please, just come to Saturday-morning service," Uncle Gabe pleads every weekend. And who am I to deny him?

We trudge off together, prayer books (the only items we're allowed to carry on the Sabbath) tucked under our arms. At the synagogue, I immediately evaluate the décor, giving points for marble columns, velvet Torah covers, anything ornate enough to compete with the ancient Greeks.

My mother had never instilled what Gabe refers to as "an interest in Judaism." In fact, I had barely known that she was Jewish, and I was certain, from her taste in men, that she was drawn to Christians, at least for romance.

Uncle Len, a devout agnostic, tries in his mild way to dissuade Gabe from the attempt at my conversion. "You've got her too late. Eight is too late," he points out. "Marx says: 'Give me the child for the first five years . . .'"

"She loves kissing the Torah" is Gabe's defense.

And indeed I do: The Torah, heavily decorated with carved silver "breastplates" and dangling what I call "jingle bells," attracts me, as any glittery artifact does. Loving ceremony of any kind, I rush to kiss the Torah (and don't tell Gabe I also enjoy communion with my friend Diana, not to mention all the voodoo rites we perform in a freelance fashion).

What I do like in *shul:* Even though the synagogue has sex segregation—men downstairs and women upstairs—Uncle Gabe obtains a dispensation, and I am allowed to remain at his side, actually under the tent of his *tallis.* Like Uncle Len, I love any disguise, and I play peekaboo with Gabe's *tallis,* while he sways in devout prayer.

What disappoints me in *shul* is the constant insistence that there is but "only one God." I think this is an admission that they are caught short; in comparison to my other religion, the Jews look a bit limited. And, if there is only one God, I bet He Is the One Who Will Punish You. The odds are better (and there is more variety and better artwork) with multiple deities. So, even as I sway under Gabe's *tallis,* and recite the holy prayers, I can't help thinking: "I want *more* gods."

Encouraged by these Saturday sessions, Gabe wants to enroll me in the Hebrew school. The school convenes every afternoon at 3:30, after what I call the "real" school lets out.

"Don't force her" is all Uncle Len will say.

I'm not eager to lose the play time—from three to six is the special part of my day when Susan and Diana come up to 7G to enact secret scenarios. . . .

We include my uncles in expurgated versions of our harem routines. Now we are rulers—Amazon queens—and my uncles are the slaves. We even have slave names for them: Len is Leonardo and Gabe is Gabrielo. Susan and I (or, on alternate afternoons, Diana and I) actually lie around on a bedspread on the living-room floor, eating bunches of grapes. (We base our performance on scenes of decadence in *The Robe*.) When we need more refreshments, we snap our fingers, and call for our menservants: "Oh, Leonardo! Gabrielo!" And my poor uncles come tottering, holding platters of cocktail frankfurters, from the kitchenette.

"You have it made here," Susan says.

Can I trade these seraglio sessions for serious Hebrew studies in the basement of the temple? I'm not too interested, but like the cunning heroine-villainess of one of my own sagas, I offer Uncle Gabe a proposition I'm sure he will refuse: I'll go to Hebrew school, if he will give me a dog.

*O*ur family doesn't have dogs," Uncle Gabe insists. Len contradicts him: the family once had a dog—a white terrier—long ago, in Russia.

Why do I want a dog?

I don't really know. None of my friends have dogs. And I have always loved cats. But there is a new trauma—a good reason to avoid felines.

"The impostor Sparkle" episode is the first disaster of our

new life in 7G. Although I now know Rosie is gone, I still try to retrieve my past. I have taken to standing outside my old apartment door, and I am once more looking for my "old" cat, the vanished Sparkle.

Some afternoons I run to 3M by mistake, the habit of four years. I stand outside the familiar door and strain to overhear the sounds of family life within. Sometimes I imagine that Rosie and I are behind the door still living our old life. A version of my "other planet" theory: I'm still not convinced that my existence with my mother isn't proceeding somewhere—on another plane, if not another planet.

When, one afternoon, I hear a high foreign whine of recrimination emanating from 3M (raised strangers' voices), I acknowledge that other people live inside. Still, I often stand there, and my uncles know where to look if they can't find me at dinnertime.

I have a new tack on the situation: I am imprinting my memories of life there. I will not forget, I must not forget. I vow to remember everything about Rosie and our life together. This pledge takes physical root in the corridor on our old hemp "welcome" mat. (I imagine that my small figure, planted there, vibrating with determination, is not a pleasant sight for the new tenants.)

In any case, my next goal is to retrieve my lost cat, the missing Sparkle. With Diana's help, I scour the parks and alleyways, mewing and calling. I leave cans of open tuna fish on the curb. There are dozens of stray cats, and as soon as I see one who remotely resembles Sparkle I seize her and cart her up to the new apartment.

Deep in my heart, I know this cat is not the real Sparkle. The real Sparkle was white, and this cat has a small circle of orange near its tail. I am willing to edit out the orange spot. I also finesse the fact that Sparkle was a female and this cat has two fuzzy balls tucked between its legs. In fact, everything about this cat—its gravelly meow, its crusted eyelids, its grungy coat—is unlike the real Sparkle.

I want to believe, however, and the impostor Sparkle is set into our new bathtub. I no sooner run the tap than the impostor flies yowling from the tub, and skitters on an insane spiral course around the apartment, spewing vomitus and diarrhea simultaneously in a long, unraveling reel of foul fluid. The impostor Sparkle is in serious shape, suffering a series of seizures that sends it, back arching, almost to the ceiling. I scream as the animal does a dance of death across our living room. In a final spasm, the cat tries to bite its own tail. Spinning in the fatal frenzy, the cat finally winds up under a dining chair, where, with one last crusted look into my eyes, it dies.

My grief is extravagant. I pace the rooms, doubled over, moaning "Sparkle, Sparkle," while the false Sparkle stiffens and stares sightlessly at my demonstrations of feeling.

Uncle Len comes upon this scene: "Oh, my God," and is left with the unpleasant task of disposing of the remains.

He weeps, too; Len is moved by the loss of any life. Together, wailing, we do an intensive cleanup before Uncle Gabe gets home.

The loss of the second Sparkle is a setback. The creature's misfortune becomes my misfortune, and I find myself shivering again at night in bed. And, instead of the usual comfort I take in sleep, I descend into a Hades of my own imaginings.

The nightmares are often the same. I am being chased by faceless individuals, who, if they catch me, will kill. I run through woods, to the edge of a cliff. . . . They are right behind me.

Usually I wake just in time, but one night "they" catch me

and I feel a knife slice into my forehead. I wake to find that my head is pressed to the metal frame of my bed, but there's small comfort in knowing this was just a dream. It's too real for me to risk its happening again.

At this time, the bogeyman (or bogeywoman, for the presence is female) also moves in to 7G, to round out our junior four. The bogeywoman, or Night Witch, as I think of her, lives in our bathroom, behind the shower curtain. She might pounce at any time, if I risk going in there without turning on the light. When she's alone inside the bathroom, she swells to even more hideous proportions—expanding to fill the entire room. With this dark, amorphous evil, hissing and heaving against the tile walls, it's no wonder I learn to hold it in until morning.

The nights have become, as Uncle Len expresses it, "increasingly rough."

For the first time in my life, I try to avoid sleep—it's too scary. I stay up in bed, reading (*Grimm's Fairy Tales*—a mistake). Uncle Len is insomniac also (and always has been; he claims *never* to sleep: "I just rest"), so we often have long talks throughout the night.

While he claims never to require sleep, Uncle Len becomes concerned that I can't sleep at my age.

"You were always a wonderful sleeper," he reminisces. "Rosie never even had to ask you to go to bed. You were there."

It's true: I always dove onto any mattress in delight. I saw sleep as my sanctuary. And now, suddenly, this comfort is denied to me, it seems permanently.

Uncle Len recalls that, when I was a baby, I liked to see pictures of puppies. Now, he tacks some five-and-dime puppy prints to my bedroom wall. He walks me from one picture to the next:

"Say goodnight to Brownie. Say goodnight to Sad-Eye. Say goodnight to Whitie. . . ."

I do take some comfort in saying goodnight to the puppy pictures, but I hint that a real puppy would be better. I suppose to erase the horror of the impostor Sparkle, and in a tradeoff with Uncle Gabe, the uncles decide that I will get a dog of my own.

And so it happens that Uncle Len and I take the subway down to a pet shop, where we find the one ultimate puppy, the one who wants to be with us—a black cocker spaniel so fat she rolls over—and duly take her back to the Bronx.

The moment our new cocker spaniel puppy looks up at Uncle Len, he makes the first of the puppy pronouncements: "This isn't an ordinary dog."

Bonny isn't ordinary. She has a liquid, intellectual gaze, as if she's not a dog but a Democrat, interested, like Gabe and Len, in civil liberties.

We gather around her cardboard box, and, as instructed, tuck her in for the night with a towel wrapped around a ticking clock. I keep her near my bed, and find immediate comfort in her presence. If I drop my hand down, she licks my fingers. I can feel her entire chubby body move, propelled by her batting tail.

When she whimpers, I lift her into my bed, and position her so her head rests on my pillow, one silken ear spread out across the case.

The next afternoon, I keep my part of the bargain. For love of my cocker spaniel, I begin Hebrew instruction. I am the only girl at the Young Israel, in a class of boys studying for their bar mitzvah. I don't understand the lessons, and the teacher, an older man named Mr. Pugatch, spends most of the session screaming at the boys in a unique and, I assume, Hebrew style: He pounds on his own bald head with both fists, yelling: "You make my blood boil, you make my blood boil."

Hebrew school isn't easy, I decide, but it's worth it.

We all fall in love with Bonny. Even Gabe admits she "has soul." She seems to fill in with spaniel sympathy whatever element was missing in our home. Soon, we have the accoutrements of dog devotion: Bonny has her own toys (Gabe's slippers), special snacks (kosher corned beef), and a secure berth in my bed (her own pillow).

It would seem our arrangements are complete, when one evening I rush home from Hebrew school to find a fourth mattress, still in brown wrapping paper, propped up outside our apartment door. Into our increasingly snug household comes a fourth member of what the uncles call "our team."

Their mother is moving in with us.

*W*hen I hear that she's coming to stay with us, I'm pleased. I think of "grandmother" as a generic brand. My friends have grandmothers who seem permanently bent over cookie racks. They are Nanas and Bubbas, sources of constant treats, huggers and kissers, pinchers of cheeks.

I have no memory of my own grandmother, who has lived in a distant state, and whom I haven't seen since I was a baby. But, with the example of the neighborhood grandmothers before me, I can hardly wait to have a grandmother of my own—and the cookies will be nice, too. For, while my uncles provide a cuisine that ranges from tuna croquettes to Swedish meatballs, they show no signs of baking anything more elegant than a potato.

My main concern on the day of my grandmother's arrival is, How soon will she start the cookies?

She arrives, flanked by Len and Gabe. Although her sons tower over her, she appears in no way diminished: she holds herself absolutely straight, and cuts a trim figure in a navy-blue hat, tailored suit, an ermine stole. She holds, tucked under her arm, a purple leather portfolio, which contains her work-in-progress, a manuscript entitled *Philosophy for Women*. She is followed by her custom-made white trunk, packed with purses, earrings, dresses, and more purple-inked pages that stress "the spiritual above the material."

At five feet one inch, she is not much taller than I am—thin and straight, with a pug nose, one brown eye (the good eye) and one blue eye (the bad eye, frosted by a cataract). Her name is "Esther in Hebrew, Edna in English, and Etka in Russian." She prefers the Russian, referring to herself as "Etka from Minsk."

It's not immediately apparent, but she is also deaf in her left ear (the bad ear) but can hear with the right (her good ear). As the good ear is on the opposite side from the good eye, anyone speaking to her must run around her in circles or sway to and fro, if eye contact and audibility are to be achieved simultaneously.

Etka from Minsk has arrived not directly from Minsk, as the black-eyed ermine stole seems to suggest, but after many moves. She enters with the draft of family scandal at her back, blown out of another relative's home after assaults upon her dignity. She holds the evidence: an empty-socketed peacock pin. My cousin, an eleven-year-old boy, has surgically plucked out the rhinestone eyes. She cannot be expected to stay where such acts occur. She has to be among "human beings," among "real people" who can understand. We seem to understand. Uncle Len, Gabe, and I encircle her, study her vandalized peacock pin, and vow that such affronts will never happen with us.

She pats my head—a good sign—and asks me to sing the Israeli national anthem. I have the impression that I am auditioning for her, and I am. I sing "Hatikvah" (off-key, but she can't quite hear me), and she gives me a dollar: a wonderful start.

Uncles Len and Gabe go off to their respective jobs, leaving me alone with Etka from Minsk for the first time. I look at her, expecting her to toss off her tailored jacket, tuck up her cuffs, and roll out the cookie dough. Instead, she purses her lips in an expression she learned as a child, and tilts her head in a practiced way: "Now, perhaps, you could fix me a little lunch?"

It isn't supposed to be this way, I think as I take her order: "toasted cheese sandwich and a sliced orange."

Together we unpack the massive white trunk. She instructs me to stack her belongings—dozens of silk blouses, custom-made suits, spectator pumps, and a queen's ransom in costume jewelry—on my bed. I'm dazzled—and dazed. It had not occurred to me that she would sleep in my room: I am eight and she is nearly eighty. But my uncles don't see the incongruity, only the affinity of sex. Now, my old room is dubbed "The Girls' Room" by Uncle Gabe.

What goes on in The Girls' Room proves the name is apt: I've acquired not the doting Nana of my dreams, but an aged kid sister. Within hours, the theft and rivalry begin.

The first night, Etka from Minsk makes an official presentation—performed as if in an operetta. She walks to the dinette in full evening dress, holding in her outstretched hands three ornate beaded evening bags. "These are the three evening bags I have saved for my three daughters-in-law."

Even I hear one false note: why does she still have three gift purses when she has only two unmarried sons? *Ah ha . . .*

"I lost one son, a war victim" is how she describes Norm's marriage to Barb. The result is now she need save only two beaded bags; it is out of the question to reward Barb with a beaded bag. Therefore, one bag is available, to be given to someone worthy of owning it. Etka's good eye seeks me out at my place at the table. She holds out the most beautiful of the evening bags: a violet flapper-style purse, with long, sparkling fringes. I am beside myself: I would rather have this shimmering accessory than a lifetime of cookies or rolled strudels.

And yes, "I am giving this beautiful beaded bag, which I had saved for my third daughter-in-law, to my only granddaughter, Lily." She pronounces my name "Leeli," adding to the foreign feel of this presentation. I love every second of the ceremony, which reminds me of tableaux depicting Indians trading for the Island of Manhattan.

I rise, bow, accept the beaded bag. I thank her, and, for free, throw in a few verses of the Hebrew national anthem.

On impulse, I rush to my room and open my treasure chest (a

lavender metal candy box), and run back with an offering of my own: my most prized piece, the ivory heart-shaped pin I had planned to give to my mother. I present this pin, with a set of matching earrings, and Etka nods. This seems appropriate. Uncle Len and Uncle Gabe exchange a glance. Gabe cannot resist saying, out of Etka's "good" earshot (the first of our many mouthed asides), "See, they're getting along beautifully." Uncle Len, in response, raises his eyebrows, Marx brothers style.

That night Etka and I share the large bedroom. (Have there ever been two more disparate partners on twin beds?)

I spy on her, through not-quite-closed eyelids, as she prepares for sleep. She wears a matched peach set of European-style underwear. Her legs are slim and well-shaped. Her entire body is, in fact, surprisingly intact. Her small breasts droop, but not much (not as much as Ava's, anyway), and her white skin appears smooth, although she wears, here and there, tiny cysts—skin cells no longer incorporated—and, near her collarbone, a small garnet brooch of blood blisters. (Soon I know her body as well as I know mine, perhaps better, as I spend more time studying hers. And, because I often escort her by the elbow, I come to know the crushed flower-petal feel of her upper arm: cool and white, like the talcum powder that sifts from her skin.)

Etka takes to her bed with my kind of enthusiasm: a haven. She turns on her side, and nuzzles deep down into her pillowcase. I envy her swift snuggle into sleep. Within seconds, she is breathing evenly. Eventually, the sound must lull me, too, although throughout the night I seem to retain an awareness of something new, an unfamiliar form in the shadowed room. This is not unpleasant, only different, and tucked tight under my pink "blanky," I pass a pretty fair night.

Which is why morning comes as such a blow. I wake and rush to my drawer to admire my new treasure, the violet beaded bag. I look through my scant possessions and there can be no doubt: the purse is missing.

Purloined. I look to my still-sleeping grandmother. Now she lies confident, on her back. On a hunch, I tiptoe to her file cabinet, and peek. Poorly concealed, under her manuscript, is a flash of violet fringe. I don't take the bag but run straight to Uncle Len, who is popping corn to accompany today's breakfast menu of tuna croquettes and baked beans. He wears his pith helmet and a professional chef's apron, over a tee-shirt and suit pants. I tell on Etka: she stole back the purse. . . .

Uncle Len doesn't look too surprised as he rattles his pressure cooker, and mini-explosions ricochet within. "Court will convene tonight" is all he says.

$\mathcal{T}$he decision goes against me. I can't believe it. They know she has that beaded bag. And, when confronted, she refuses to give it (or the ivory pin and earring set) back to me. They admit this is unfair, but they ask me to forbear: they don't want to upset Etka so early in her stay.

I burn at the injustice of it, and feel the heat of an uncomfortable truth: where once I had my uncles' undivided indulgence, they are now split as my grandmother and I vie for their attention. The household, formerly geared to my little-girl needs, is now rearranged to accommodate hers.

The crimes continue—I suffer serious affronts. Etka, in a fit of frugality, scissors all the household blankets, including "Blanky," in half. "Now," she says, her good eye gleaming, "we have twice as many."

I lie under my narrow slice of blanket and stare up at the ceiling. I think evilly of ways of getting Etka from Minsk out of the apartment.

Matters worsen, as more and more of my trinkets disappear. One afternoon, I come home to find Etka squeezed into my unbuttoned favorite blouse. Rouged and beribboned, she insists the size 3 blouse is hers.

Meanwhile, I am forced to adapt to her idiosyncrasies. She covers everything black—from the telephone to the dog—with white doilies. She leaves saucers balanced on top of glasses. She tries to lock Bonny out of the apartment.

"Black, black, you never get back," she chants. In Russia, her family had a white dog, which was kept in its own room, a white room. The dog's name had been Belka, which means "white" in Russian.

"We had a white dog," she says, as if that's that.

She also sings nonstop—Russian, Hebrew, and German songs. Then, in a tuneless monotone, she chants her own praises. She often takes both parts in a dialogue: "Who is the most beautiful, intelligent woman in the world? I am. Who has the most distinguished family? Who has the most perfect legs?" She does, she does.

One afternoon, as we sit by the window (where she loves to watch the neighbors in disapproval), she announces for the hundredth time, "Once a beauty, always a beauty." Something in me snaps—she's wearing my pin, my earrings, my blouse, and has been bragging for days. I say, with a child's cruel honesty: "You have wrinkles."

To me her face appears creased, as if she has pressed herself against the mesh of a window screen. Etka doesn't see herself that way. She purses her lips, exaggerating the "whistle marks," and laughs as if what I've said is absurd. "Once a beauty, always a beauty," she insists.

This stream of egotism would be intolerable—if she sounded sure. But even an eight-year-old can hear a tinny ring.

The word that Uncle Len uses to explain Etka from Minsk's behavior is "arteriosclerosis." He tells me that sometimes not enough blood reaches Etka's brain, and she "forgets."

She forgets so much that sometimes she locks me out of the apartment. Other times she greets me by saying, "You look familiar." Sitting in our room, she asks, "What hotel is this?"

My answer, shouted into her good ear, is "This isn't a hotel. This is our apartment." Her response is another hoot of laughter: "Then why are we in the ballroom?"

In "the ballroom," one afternoon, I dance my old harem dance, wearing what little jewelry I can still find and a bath towel. "Very nice," she says.

But sex is on her mind, too. She tumbles out of bed one night, thrown by a nightmare that her sons are marrying "tramps." Uncle Len and Gabe must help me lift Etka into her bed. All the while they reassure her: "We aren't marrying tramps." She points to a red night light that glows near her bed: "Then what's that for?"

They buy a bed with crib bars—a hospital model that adjusts to full and semi recline, the better to secure Etka from her increasingly frequently apparitions. On most afternoons, an elderly woman, Mrs. Mark, is hired to mind my grandmother until I can return from school. This woman soon enters Etka's nightmares as a new persona: "I saw a blonde in a fur coat in here," she cries in the middle of the night.

I try to explain. That wasn't a blonde in a fur coat, that was another eighty-year-old woman, with yellowing white hair, wearing a fake mouton jacket. She'll have none of that: "I saw her, I saw that tramp, that bum in her fur coat."

When Mrs. Mark returns for the next grandmother-sitting session, we all hold our breath. Apparently Etka holds her tongue. In fact, when being cared for, she has all her senses. "Oh, you're so wonderful," she coos to "the tramp."

More of my clothes disappear. She has almost everything now. I have no necklaces—she's wearing them—and everything pink is also appropriated. My uncles keep replacing items only to see them disappear the next night.

Finally, we fight: arm-to-arm combat. I'm shocked at her grip, steely as the bars that lock her into bed at night. Her good eye burns into mine and she says, "I'll tell."

And she does. For the first time I'm scolded. She turns their love to disapproval, and, oh, how it chafes.

I throw a tantrum—the first under the uncle regime—and they stand by, helpless, as I pound the abraded floor with my fists.

That night, Etka from Minsk has a new nightmare. She

screams, and I wake up . . . to hear her crying: "Where is my baby? Where is my baby?"

*A*n eighty-year-old woman is dreaming that she has just given birth. Now she can't find the baby. She thrashes in bed, lifting her sheets: "Where is my baby? Where is my baby?"

I try to comfort her: there is no baby. "You were asleep," I tell her.

No, she insists: the baby was "just here" in the bed. Etka from Minsk starts to cry. I run to the other rooms and alert my uncles. Uncle Gabe, in striped pajamas, and Uncle Len, in tee-shirt and shorts, rush into The Girls' Room.

To prove there is no baby, we lift her mattress. There we discover a new secret: Etka's life savings, bound in a knotted lisle stocking, a wad of single bills, that she calls her *"knippl."* Also: my stolen necklaces, cultured pearls, and pink hair ribbons.

It takes hours to convince Etka that she has not given birth and somehow misplaced her newborn baby. We usher her into the present. Uncle Len whispers her life history: "You had five babies, but that was a long time ago. . . ."

My uncles also bring me up to date. At the time when my grandmother had her children, women gave birth at home. Although my uncles, as young boys, were locked out of her bedroom, they heard her scream when their youngest brother was born. They tell me that babies were often kept, for the first few months, in the mother's bed. They believe that Etka's nightmare is a reprise of past maternal anxiety, suffered, most likely, after childbirth.

I say nothing, but I have my own theory. I believe Etka cries for her lost daughter, my mother. By day, my grandmother will not admit that Rosie has died. "My daughter was given a wonderful job. She's in Washington" is all my grandmother will say. She incorporates this mythical promotion into her bragging monologues: "They don't promote just anyone's daughter, they promote *my* daughter. . . ."

There is much precedent in the family for pretending that the dead have not died but are living in other cities. Practicing a form of emotional etiquette, it is considered good form to spare elderly relatives sad news. Whenever we attend family reunions, the uncles give me a quick refresher course in who's officially dead and who's not. It would be helpful to maintain a cross-index, because some elderly aunts know while others don't know. Great-aunt Becky believes she has a nephew in Alaska, while her sister, Berta, knows that nephew died of heart failure three years ago. Entire sections of the family (the Kroll branch) have expired, but their surviving sister, my grandmother, has been told the whole group "moved to California." (When a cousin actually did move to California, no one believed it—the other cousins all believed this was a euphemism for the much-longer journey.)

My grandmother had been spared the news of Rosie's death

for several months, but an aunt finally told. Etka did not acknowledge the death, however, and she maintained the Washington myth for another few months. I sensed she knew the truth but
chose not to say so. When someone said the name Rosie, she
would turn pale.

The way my grandmother mourns for my mother is something I understand. I recognize her nightmare, too. We both
know the Night Witch may hide behind our closed closet door,
filling all shadows by assuming new, awful shapes. When Etka insists her baby is stolen, I secretly agree.

Over the next several nights, I lull my own fear by comforting Etka. If I can tuck her under the covers, and sing her to sleep,
maybe everything will be all right.

Uncle Len tells me that my grandmother's distaste for the
color black has nothing to do with disliking the dog or being
racist. She fears death so much she cannot cope with the color of
mourning.

After that explanation, I keep the doily over the telephone,
never wear black, and put a red collar on the dog (to minimize the
effect). As time passes, my grandmother's night panics become
less frequent, and I take a certain pleasure in offering her the reas-
surance she needs. "Who is the smartest, most beautiful woman in
the world?" she asks.

I know the answer, and she knows enough to laugh.

"You are!"

*O*ur rivalry mellows into conspiracy. Within months we find uses for each other. I provide her with lunches and secret, forbidden ice-cream sundaes. She rewards me with cold cash. She continues to steal my clothes. I start to charge her competitive prices.

We work out elaborate professional schemes. She gives me my first paying job: I am the official editor of her memoirs, *Philosophy for Women*. My grandmother and I have an actual contract—drawn up and witnessed by my uncles (Gabe is her attorney, Len is my counsel). For $25, "Miss Shaine agrees to edit and type fifty copies of Mrs. Etka Kroll Shaine's book, *Philosophy for Women*." This document is finalized with a homemade notary stamp, and sealed with Sabbath candle wax.

"I'm making a fortune," I think, until I'm deep into the work: *Philosophy for Women* fills more than a hundred spiral pad notebooks, and is written in Etka's inimitable style. Every sentence begins "I believe," abbreviated in the final thirty notebooks to "I.B." She capitalizes every word and her spelling is an almost unmeetable challenge for a fourth grader. She spells "actions" as "actshuns," "young" as "jong," and "silence" as "silens." A sample sentence: "When I was jong, there were many actshuns what I dint approve from, but I sofr'd in silens." The memoir is propelled along with the same momentum as her in-person monologues: "I had great courage, also beauty. . . ."

The theme of *Philosophy for Women*, if it can be summed up, is that she was right not to do housework. She I.B.s that women are made for higher things than cooking and cleaning. She had cleaned her home once, and realized that wasn't for her. The occasion was dramatic. She was a bride, and she lived in four newly decorated rooms: "One was covered in wine-color silk, with a wine-color carpet, the other room was blue, with blue silk wallpaper, the kitchen was yellow, and the living room was white. . . ."

I.B. it took her an entire day to dust these four rooms, and when she was finished, she lay down in the center of the living-room floor: "I.B. not to disturb anything." She was so exhausted she fell asleep, and her husband (who also "B." in higher and higher education) returned home to find her. He panicked, thinking she had died. They both decided, on the spot, that she should never do housework again, but should do only "brainwork."

This scene is the climax to a hundred thousand words of "philosophy" justifying her decision, and she is backed up with liberal quotes from Spinoza, Kant, Plato, Albert Einstein, Eleanor Roosevelt, and others. She also includes "*mein ohn* quotations."

As we work, night after night, transcribing this manuscript, I make an occasional editorial suggestion: "I don't think you can have your own quotations. I think 'quotations' mean other people said that."

"I have *mein ohn* quotations" is Etka's only response. I decide to do what any editor would with an obstinate writer who will not back down: "Leave it in, for the time being."

Uncle Len gives me my first typewriter—for this project. Soon I have my own work-in-progress—the "autobiography" of Pocahontas. The premise of my novel, *I, Pocahontas:* the heroine returns to Manhattan in a time machine. She has a series of adventures that illustrate how much Manhattan has changed since the 1600s.

I mentally shift gears every evening to commute between these two works. Both Etka and I experience the euphoria of the writer's trance. We are finally underway. "This is what I always wanted to do," Etka confirms, "not housework."

My grandmother's true nature—her high spirits—emerge and I learn: she can get away with anything, as long as she enjoys doing it. Her relentless enjoyment of herself makes her fun to be with, and soon she includes me in her monologues: "And I have a dear, fine, distinguished granddaughter, who also B. in higher and higher education."

Her temper squalls are infrequent but spring up, like tornadoes, without warning. One afternoon I come home to find her walking agitated circles near the window.

What's wrong? Has something happened?

She won't answer. She shakes her head. What's the use? This is too terrible, a problem past solutions. An incurable ache. She begins to "oikah" ("oikah" is a verb in our home, applicable when someone, usually Etka, begins to repeat "oy-yoy-yoy" by the hour).

"Oy, yoy, yoy, yoy, yoy."

"Vat? Vat?" I speak in her accent when she's distressed. "Vat's the matter?"

It's hopeless, is all she will confide. The one thing in the entire world that she would really like to have and she can never have it. I imagine, at first, that she wants more costume jewelry, perhaps the birthday ring my uncles have given me. Or, perhaps, my new pink princess dress?

No. No. I should know better. This is "not material."

What, then? A white dog—a "Belka"?

No, Belka was nice, but now she says that Bonny, the black dog, is acceptable. In fact, Bonny sits by her side, offering cocker condolence, as she says this. Etka routinely tosses her hunks of challah. They have achieved a *rapprochement.* She still objects to "black, black, you never get back," but Bonny is often disguised—wearing what Uncle Gabe calls a "sport jacket" (a blue plaid dog coat, selected by Gabe for this purpose, which, when worn belted, gives Bonny a stocky, Scottish look).

Knowing Etka's passion for "white, white," I try again. I recall, in her attraction toward anything white, she once pointed to a white Jaguar, parked on the street, and told Len and Gabe to get it for her. They told her they would love to buy her the white Jaguar, but pointed out that no one in the family could drive. That didn't matter. She kept repeating, "white, *weissa, weissa.*" We could buy it, and she could sit in it, on the street.

I remind her of the white Jaguar. No, she says—I told you this is not material. In one of her sudden seizures of despair, Etka waves a hand, dismissing all cars on the street, all cars in the world, even white ones. What good can a car do her now? When she doesn't have the "one thing that really matters."

What? *Vat?*

"I.B.," she says at last, "I am nothing without a college diploma." This is the first time, the only time, I ever see Etka weep. Her good eye and her opaque eye, both stream tears of profound regret.

College diplomas do not come up coincidentally in our apartment. The walls are now lined with them. Uncle Gabe and Uncle Len's college diplomas, even their high school diplomas, are framed and mounted on the walls of The Girls' Room. Etka loves to look at them. She has had a photo montage constructed of her sons wearing caps and gowns.

Even as she weeps, Etka is preparing to hang the next graduation picture. Uncle Len has been slipping off to night school, and has earned the final credits for a master's degree. The next week, at age forty-one, he will participate in the group graduation ceremonies at NYU Uptown. We are all attending his graduation. Etka has a new white dress and a white straw hat, and I have already polished her spectator pumps.

Thrilled as she is to celebrate her son's "higher and higher achievements," she cannot help wishing it were possible for her to be graduated also, and to receive a diploma. Her mood deepens as the event approaches, and by the time the day arrives for the ceremony, I sense Etka is running a higher and higher emotional temperature.

The event is one of our few public outings as a complete family group. Len, Gabe, Etka, and I take a taxi—an event in itself (the last time Etka climbed into a taxicab was when she moved in with us).

During the ride, Etka recites the glories of Len's past academic achievements, which are, in fact, pretty impressive: "My dear, fine, distinguished son was the youngest [jongest] ever to graduate from City College. . . ." His I.Q. is over two hundred. Somehow, in Etka's mind, this has to do with "his high forehead." And now, on this day, after years of discreet night-time study, Uncle Len will receive the highest awards: He is being graduated, according to Etka: "magna, summa, summa cum laude." She can hardly wait to get his diploma, but her voice catches each time on the word "diploma."

At the outdoor ceremony, most of the graduates are in their twenties, and the spectators, sitting on folding chairs, are primarily matched sets of parents. Uncle Len appears as different from his fellow grads as we do from the other families. He towers, taller than usual, in his rented mortarboard cap and sweeping black-and-purple gown (Etka wants to keep the outfit: she even unfurls her tightly rolled *knippl* to pay, a rare extravagance).

Uncle Len is so tall his graduation robes don't quite clear his calves. And his giant "detective" shoes flash, professionally shined. He is two decades older and a foot taller than many of the students at his side.

In the family gallery, Uncle Gabe, wearing a vintage serge suit, my grandmother in her white outfit, with the ermine stole (tossed on for emphasis, despite the June heat), and I—in pink taffeta—must appear as unlikely as Uncle Len in this crowd.

As we watch, Uncle Len strides to the podium. Because I have been somewhat numbed by Etka's incessant bragging, I'm surprised that something she has said is true: Uncle Len is being graduated as first in his class. The actual presentation leaves even Etka speechless—she is more accustomed to filling in the blanks. Now that her son has actually been honored, she can't speak. Finally, she manages to whisper: "Who do they give the biggest prize to? *Mein* son."

Mein is still the mainstay of her vocabulary, but as Len and Gabe escort Etka across the grassy graduation field, she confesses "*mein* sorrow." What she suffers in silence (*silens*) is that she will never answer to her name being called from a platform, never walk to the podium, never wear the cap and gown . . . never (she begins to *oikah*) . . . hold in her own hands a roll of parchment that proves she can do brainwork.

Uncle Len stops in midstride and whips off his cap and gown. We all help Etka into the outfit. She stops oiking at once, and says, "A picture, a picture."

That graduation picture is only a stopgap measure. The need for her own diploma has taken a deeper root in Etka's subconscious. In her sleep she moans for her own diploma, with her own name on it.

Within days we see that this is an obsession; it will not go away. We need a real diploma for her. Uncle Len and I draw up the document, complete with fake seal and tinfoil stars for excellence. Len and I agree she must be graduated "magna, summa, magna cum laude," but late at night, after Etka has retired to her uneasy dreams of college, we debate which academic institution should award her degree.

I campaign for Columbia because she sings "Columbia, the Gem of the Ocean." Len wants her to be a Hunter grad. Uncle Gabe, of course, favors a religious institution, and is pushing Yeshiva College. We compromise: Etka will be awarded a Bachelor of Arts from Hunter *and* Columbia, with an honorary degree from Yeshiva College, as well.

We spend a few nights at the dinette table, drawing up additional prizes for "special achievements in her field." Then, at last, in lieu of a college campus, we decide to stage the graduation in our local park, Joyce Kilmer. For added drama, we hold the ceremony at night.

While we are playful in our preparations, we also know the stakes are high. Our act will have to be convincing to satisfy Etka from Minsk. We cannot fail—a lifetime of oiking will be the penalty.

And so, on an early summer evening, we escort Etka to the

civilized park on Grand Concourse. We have deliberately chosen this park, for the benches are packed with spectators. On hot nights, the entire neighborhood turns out. In fact, this park is more popular by night than by day, perhaps because the street lamps provide a more pleasing light than the noontime sun, which seems to bake one into the pavement.

On this night, the street lamps cast haloes. The entire park gives off a phosphorescent glow. The maple trees, wearing their urban metal corsets, take on some midsummer night's magic. Backlit, the leaves show their green veins, and look more verdant than they do by day.

The elderly men and women are lined up on benches. "The jury," Etka calls them, in a whisper in my ear, as we walk past. In this artificial light, each white-haired head seems to wear a corona. They do appear to be elder statesmen and women, in some science-fiction jury of the future. They eye Etka, dressed in her best white nautical-trim suit, the spectator pumps, clutching a good purse, and my uncles, overdressed in suits for a summer night, and me, back in the pink taffeta dress. Along with Etka, I sense a judgment—perhaps not entirely favorable—is being passed.

Etka draws herself up—her already erect posture becomes even more imposing. She is ready to defend herself. Although no one makes an adverse remark, Etka whispers, "Take it from whom it comes." Curiosity is a kind of condemnation: we all feel that.

She's been fighting "them" for decades, without elaborating on who "they" are—those who promote housework and oppose education.

We flank her: Gabe on one side, Len and I on the other. The dog, Bonny, leads, straining as I hold her leash. She has a feral side that emerges in any park, even a flat, cemented park, where the trees wear metal girdles. Twin red lights ignite in her eyes, like high beams, and she seems focused for a hunt.

Gabe, always a campaigner for personal freedom, gives the order: "Let her loose." And Bonny takes off, leash trailing (so Uncle Len can step on it, if need be, to yank her back to our "civilization"). We allow Bonny a few frenzied circular runs, until, winded, she can behave decorously enough to join us for the main event: the ceremony.

We have preselected the Joyce Kilmer plaque—"I think that I shall never see / A poem lovely as a tree" —as the optimum location for the presentation. We feel Joyce Kilmer lends an academic sanction to the proceedings. We've eliminated the only other choice—the mermaid fountain—because of the bare marble breasts (inappropriate, and Etka might object—"Tramps") and the dedication to Heine (too German for Etka from Minsk). We could have tied into the Yankees connection, so prevalent here, but we thought the baseball statuettes would seem to make sport of this occasion.

As we gather in a semicircle, in front of the Kilmer memorial, Uncle Len announces our purpose for Etka: "We are gathered here tonight on this the third day of July, for a special, *private*..." No one can weigh a word like Len. "...a private graduation for a student who has achieved the highest honors in her class...."

Etka looks surprised but not askance. She inhabits a world where such events are not entirely unexpected (arteriosclerosis has its rewards, screening disclaimers and editing out the unpleasant). Uncle Gabe proffers the mortarboard, with white tassel (white, white, *"weissa, weissa"*), and produces a white graduation robe from a supermarket shopping bag. I assist Etka in donning the robe, not an easy task, as for this occasion she has added a mink stole ("not first-quality mink," she always says of this garment, which is actually muskrat, a word she won't say. . . . She prefers instead to describe this fur as "second-quality mink").

The effect is oddly dignified. Etka assumes her most practiced serious expression, in which she purses her lips and looks downward, an expression which she says all girls were taught in Russia, and in which she has instructed me—"It will make you look intelligent."

Toeing out in her brown-and-white spectator pumps, my grandmother takes a few measured steps up to Uncle Len, and bows her head as she accepts the diploma. As Uncle Len recites her "achievements," Uncle Gabe whips out more documentation—forged letters from President Eisenhower (although we all preferred the man he defeated, Adlai Stevenson), and Dr. Belkin, the president of Yeshiva College. Then Uncle Len produces the ultimate, a surprise "recommendation, commendation" from Etka's personal heroine, Eleanor Roosevelt. This unlikely letter states: "I too raised five children, and know you are a fine, distinguished mother, who believes in higher and higher education."

And the final highest honor: the prize awarded to Etka Kroll Shaine for distinguished work in her field, philosophy.

The graduation is instantly celebrated with refreshments: orange-and-vanilla Humorettes. The nocturnal Good Humor man materializes, a vision in his white uniform, his wagon giving off a visible frost, tinkling jingle bells—like an emissary from a good dream.

This night is what Etka calls "a highlight from *mein* life." The diploma becomes her most prized possession—more valued even than the violet beaded bag (which she still periodically presents to me, only to retrieve later, under cover of darkness).

Her diploma, which Len has framed, under glass, doesn't hang on the wall. No, it means so much to Etka that she usually holds it in her lap, or props it up on the windowsill, where she can gaze at it and her own partial reflection, in long afternoon sessions of self-admiration.

*H*umming, chanting, and gazing at the diploma, Etka can have good moods that endure for months. But I soon learn that she can throw a fit faster than I can, if provoked. She shows a new side when I tell her that Uncle Len has been having an affair.

I confide this information in all innocence. She has a repeat chorus that bemoans, "Two sons, O.B.s" (old bachelors). Oh, why, she cries, can't they meet women and marry?

Happy to reassure her, I tell her Uncle Len has a steady girl-friend, a woman he sleeps with every Saturday night.

Her tongue turns black, and she falls to the floor. From then on, on Saturday nights, she can be counted on to throw a spell. Her technique is impressive: She can actually do a death rattle, at will. "Don't go," she says . . . then the rattle. When Len promises to stay, Etka's rattle subsides, and she's soon up and around, chortling and singing: "I.B. two fine, distinguished sons should not be O.B.s."

But try to get out of the house.

Uncle Len, who already seems to be incognito, becomes even more elusive when leaving the premises. He glides out the door, after Etka has retired for the evening, and reappears at dawn. "Don't tell," he whispers.

I don't.

It's easy to deceive Etka. If she does wake up and Len is missing, I can say, "He's gone to the library," and she will never question it.

Our household revolves around such incidents. If tragedy has brought us together, it's comedy that keeps us close. I decide that my grandmother won't be so jealous if she has a love interest of her own. I invent a character known as The Professor, who sends Etka "love letters." In a cramped, forged handwriting, I write to her as The Professor, to plead his case:

"I have heard you are a fine, educated woman. I love you from afar. . . ."

Although she protests—"I loved only once"—Etka can't wait to receive the next letter from The Professor. She dictates long responses, giving him tastes of her *Philosophy for Women,* and thanking him politely for his interest. She can't meet him, she explains, but how about sending a picture?

We develop other routines for my uncles' entertainment at dinner. Etka sits at her place and sighs, "Alone is a stone." This is my cue to enter, as her long-lost friend.

I hobble in, supported by Uncle Len's walking stick (one of his mysterious props). In character, I am elaborately costumed and made-up: I wear one of Etka's dresses (she has some pretty snappy sailor suits, custom-made), her spectator pumps, and seamed stockings. My hair is heavily powdered with baby talcum, and I wear dark red lipstick and two high spots of rouge.

"Ha-lo, Etka . . ." I begin, speaking in her accent, "I happen to be in the neighborhood, and I thought I'd drop by . . ."

"Who invited her?" my grandmother would cackle to my uncles. Then, with perfect, phony manners: "Please, sit down . . ." While I chat, Etka gives comic asides to her audience: "Make a party, they'll come. . . ." When I finally get up to leave, she stage-whispers: "They're so jealous they can't stand to see me here . . . they can't stand to see somebody better than themselves. . . ."

I.B. our little drama is an accurate reprise of my grandmother's hostile relations with her sister-in-law. Etka had married a handsome man—his photograph shows a dignified giant (not unlike Len) wearing rimless glasses and a dreamy expression (not unlike Gabe's). This man, her husband, Josef, was the darling brother of six accomplished sisters, all of whom prided themselves on being *baleboostehs*. "I hate even the word," Etka spits. *"Baleboosteh." Hiss.* These women engaged in heavy-duty baking competitions, presenting each other with increasingly complicated braided babkas. They could not understand (or tolerate)

Etka. "Education, education," they sneered. "Education, education, but they eat *crap.*"

Her husband apparently did not care: he had married Etka to share her interests. He was also a writer, well-known in his village in Russia. His short story ("The Rock") concerning spirits trapped inside a giant boulder, at a mysterious place outside town, has been reprinted and translated into English, and is part of our family bibliography.

Recounting their courtship brings a shine to my grandmother's good eye: "I was an O.M. [old maid]—thirty and not married. I had younger sisters, who could not marry until I did—it was the custom. So that my younger sisters could marry, I began to see men. I never liked the idea to be married, to do housework. I knew five languages. Why should I do housework?"

Josef took one look at her and then ran to a photograph of her on the wall. He pointed to the photo and said, "If I can't marry this girl, I will never marry."

And so Etka married Josef, and, according to *Philosophy for Women,* and her own reports, they loved each other very much. "He knew how to pick," she says, giving him the highest accolade in the Etka repertoire. "He knew how to pick."

I too know how to pick. Soon I come to take as much comfort as she does in our nightly exchange of endearments: *"Ya tebya lyublyu," "Ya tebya tozhe lyublyu"*—"I love you," "I love you, too."

If I sell my grandmother blouses and baubles, maybe she gives me the truth in exchange. One night, when we are alone in The Girls' Room, she turns to me, suddenly lucid, her good eye as bright as it will ever be—a look I somehow recognize as her real gaze—and says: "My life passes like a dream."

When Etka meets my friends Diana and Susan, she gives them the same credit she gave her husband: "You know how to pick." With Diana, my grandmother becomes suspicious of her "Christian" appearance. Etka squints and asks Diana in a polite tone: "Are you a ham girl?"

Etka means no offense, and when Diana says "Yes," she is "a ham girl," my grandmother simply resumes her "you know how to pick" theme.

Diana, however, is also picking up on the religious difference. While I now attend Young Israel, Diana is hanging out with a bunch of older "kids," blond boys with the first blush of acne, and she runs to me with her first report of anti-Semitism.

"Is it true? Did you kill Christ and eat him for Passover?"

As always, feeling that I am lying even when telling the truth—why do I feel guilty on this one?—I deny it: "We did not."

Diana takes a historic pause, and I sense our future hangs in the eventual outcome of her thought process. Her blue eyes, flecked with flurries of white, stare into mine. At last she says with finality: "I believe you."

We are still friends, but logistics come between us. Diana is transferred from my class to a special room for disturbed children. I want to go with her, but Miss Eisen insists I remain in my own class.

Miss Eisen herself is a grown-up friend for me. Every morning I run to her classroom, eager to paint Phaeton, in his chariot, racing toward the sun. We talk about Greek gods while we paint, applying primary colors to the cardboard mural, which is taking as long as the ceiling of the Sistine Chapel to complete. Miss Eisen, a beautiful blonde who turns pink in her enthusiasms, adds fuel to my already flaming interest in Aphrodite, the Goddess of Love.

On one of these mornings, I get the inspiration: Miss Eisen can marry my uncle Gabe.

I can imagine them as a couple. She is as excitable as he is. She has a similar singing style: she belts out "When you walk through a storm, keep your chin up high. . . . You'll never walk alone" every Wednesday at assembly. She also performs a number called "Scarlet Ribbons," which features an adult tiptoeing into a child's bedroom (the child has been missing or dying), and is reassured to find this little girl sleeping in her own bed . . . with scarlet ribbons. "Scarlet ribbons, in her hair . . ."

As Miss Eisen acts out this song on the stage of P.S. 35, I can easily transport her mentally to my own apartment. She says goodnight to Uncle Gabe, then tiptoes to my room. . . .

Without permission, or even his knowledge, I take one of Gabe's song sheets and forge an impassioned message to Miss

Eisen on the border: "I would love to marry you. Will you have dinner with me?" That morning, before dipping my brush into the yellow (for Phaeton's chariot), I slip Miss Eisen the stolen sheet music for Gabe's "Love Is a River"—"While by your side . . . I stumble . . . a . . . long."

Miss Eisen colors—brighter than the flesh tint she is using on Phaeton himself. "Oh," she whispers, half to herself, "I should have realized . . ."

That afternoon she gives the song sheet back to me with a delicately penned note to Gabe, which I read in the elevator at AnaMor Towers: "Thank you so much for your interest, but I cannot accept your lovely proposal. I am already engaged."

When Uncle Gabe finds this message, now attached to the song, he accepts it in his usual spirit: "It's all right. I've learned to thrive on rejection."

*A*s a family, we are entering our golden time. Our household is as cheerful as the one I shared with Rosie. We are all busily engaged—we have our "writing hour" every night, before we go off to sleep.

Because we have no traditional seating arrangement in our living room, we tend to cluster in the orange-and-pink dinette, or lounge on our beds. It seems logical to wear bedclothes: the usual scene is Etka and I, in matching flannel nightgowns, and the uncles in robes and slippers. If Len is still cooking, he will also wear the pith helmet or, on special occasions, a navy admiral's hat. ("I'm in the galley," he'll call from the stove, where he tends his pressure cooker.)

Cooking aromas always waft through the air, as Uncle Len seems to have something "working" twenty-four hours a day. He even has a special meat-and-potato dish, a Russian recipe, known as "cholent," that calls for a twenty-four-hour baking period. A savory steam perfumes the dinette area, where Gabe always sits, bent over his poems and journal. I peek over his shoulder one night and am surprised to see that Gabe writes in the third person, in the format of a eulogy: "They will say of him that Gabe was obsessed with . . ."

Meanwhile, across the table, I may put aside a chapter— "Pocahaontas Goes to Macy's"—to work with Etka on her essay "How I Broke My Health." I know, at some point, before she lived with us, she had a fall and broke her leg. For some reason, whenever I write "I broke my health," I imagine Etka taking her own leg and snapping it, like kindling, over her opposite knee. "I.B. What Kant Said—If you break your health, you must suffer in silens."

Uncle Len can never be observed writing (he writes at "another location," never disclosed), but he often edits his own work, with us, at the table. He has a massive manuscript on the Lincoln administration, written from Secretary of War Stanton's point of view. "No one gives Stanton enough credit."

This tome represents Len's serious, academic work. Hoping "to make money," he turns out short stories, always featuring dashing men in trenchcoats, who arrive at exotic locations (usually in the Caribbean) to rescue damsels in distress. His heroes and heroines all have names like Bosco Biltwell and Gladys Glitz. In each story, the hero uncovers an unscrupulous intrigue and exposes corruption. He then whisks the damsel off to yet another exotic location, where she tells him he is wonderful.

"Well, thank you," Bosco Biltwell replied, looking down shyly, unable to stare directly into Gladys Glitz's intelligently flecked hazel eyes, "but I was more than gratified to be at your service. You owe me no more remuneration than that kiss you just so kindly planted on my left cheek." And with that Bosco Biltwell and Gladys Glitz boarded a seaplane for the Isle of Morada.

"I know this is just commercial work," Len will confess at an after-dinner reading (looking down shyly), "but I expect this may just bail us out of some financial deep waters."

"I.B. you should aim higher and higher" is Etka's critique.

"Don't sell yourself short," advises Gabe.

Diverting as these evenings are, we also enjoy our weekend excursions. Following in my mother's tradition, we go forth every Sunday to explore a new location.

In the summer we go to the city beaches—including the notorious Orchard Beach (known as Horseshit Beach for obvious reasons: the waterfront is crowded with mounted police, who gallop among the disorderly swimmers to "keep the peace").

The city beaches look like Baghdad: almost no visible sand,

only miles of people. Even the water feels crowded. If I dive under, I usually hit someone's legs, or at least suffer a close call. At the most populated beaches, the human wave seems to meet the surf, diminishing the impact of the sea. We wade into an urban ocean, the tired tide tugging at thousands of ankles.

On these outings, my uncles always wear the same clothes they wear to work: saggy suits and shined street shoes. They don't seem to own any casual outfits, but they wear bathing trunks underneath. Their heavy shoes come in handy as anchors to hold down the corners of our beach blanket. Len's side, held down under his size 13 cordovans, is particularly secure. Sea breezes never lift our blanket, while other families' blankets billow in the breeze.

My uncles have different excursion styles: Gabe charges the surf, lifts me high in the waves. Uncle Len always positions himself on the blanket and never takes off his hat and sunglasses ("I'll just oversee the situation from here").

We pack elaborate picnics, with Len's homemade treats, including his specialties: cold tuna croquettes, prepacked on paper plates. In his usual inventive way, Len has also figured out how to provide kosher hot dogs for Uncle Gabe: he has the franks swimming in boiled water, inside a Thermos bottle. "A Thermos keeps water hot" is Len's summation; "why shouldn't it keep frankfurters hot?"

Our journeys to these beaches take several hours, in transit alone, but the summer subway seems a part of the adventure. The train to Brighton Beach and Far Rockaway has straw seats, and the wicker weave lends a tropical air. I always fall asleep, smelling straw, feeling wet sand in my pants, during the long, rocking ride home.

*U*ncle Gabe often speaks in sports metaphors. And why not? We are only a fly ball away from Yankee Stadium. "Life," he says, "deals some fast balls."

Fast balls . . . Two strike-outs. Within a few short weeks after that golden summer I lose my two best friends. "One right after the other," I tell my uncles.

"That's how it often happens," Uncle Len confirms.

The first to go: Susan. In a strange reprise of the previous summer afternoon, when I lost Rosie, I am with Susan when the fast ball hits. We are playing a game on her parents' bed. Whoever can jump the highest and claim the bed as her own is King of the Mattress.

"I am the King of the Mattress," Susan is shouting. "I am the King of the Mattress."

My role is to unseat her. I take a series of sweated dives at her ankles, always being knocked back down to the floor. We have been playing for too long, and are as punchy as burned-out boxers. Sweating and screaming—Susan is even laughing and peeing in hysterical squirts at her own antics.

We hear her mother scream from the living room—assume, incorrectly, that she is going to descend on us in a fury. All afternoon we have been minded by Mr. Hassan, a man who has always been the ideal sitter—he sleeps in his recliner in the living room.

The quality of Mrs. Hassan's scream is new. Susan and I run out to the living room to see—

Mrs. Hassan is crouched over Mr. Hassan, who has slid from his recliner onto the wall-to-wall carpeting, and has turned blue.

I have a sense to preserve his privacy. I try not to look, but see his arm, twitching on its own, hitting the leg of the coffee table, as if in an automatic gesture: Keep away. Keep away . . .

Susan's mother throws the window open and wails out to the street for "Help!" On instinct I flee, run up to 7G and tell Gabe, who runs out to the street. The neighbors are hanging from the windows of AnaMor Towers. The ambulance is said to be on its way. . . .

By the time the ambulance arrives, Mr. Hassan lies dead, still wearing his plaid sport shirt and dark pants. (It amazes me for some reason that a dead person still wears the same outfit. How can it be that he dressed himself that morning, did up buttons and pulled zippers, and now no longer exists?)

Gabe is weeping. He has knocked on the doors of doctors' offices. "No one will come." In a recurrence of death etiquette, this time Gabe takes Susan with me to our apartment, while Mrs. Hassan makes arrangements.

Susan attends her father's funeral the next day. She rushes back to my apartment to tell me that her mother threw herself into the coffin. "My father looked very handsome," she reports, as objective-sounding as a journalist. "He wore a *tallis*. Everyone said he looked like he was going to his bar mitzvah."

No sooner is Mr. Hassan buried than Mrs. Hassan is on the warpath. She has never approved of me, but I am unprepared for the white-eyed glare—pure hate—that she directs at me each time we pass in the hall.

Why does she hate me? It doesn't make sense, but I know she blames me for her husband's death.

He always liked me.

Now, Mrs. Hassan hates me more than ever. "You should be taken out of that home," she says. "Look at you."

I look—I know she doesn't like the way I dress—the short, wrinkled, dye-stained clothes. And my hair—"Comb it." But I never knew the depths of her disapproval until now.

"My mother says I can't play with you anymore," Susan says one afternoon, retrieving all her love comics. "Do you want to know why?"

I don't want to know why, but I ask: "Why?"

"Because she says you live in a crazy house."

I'm so hurt I can't breathe. Susan puts her arm around me, and tells me she's leaving AnaMor Towers "anyway."

"I'm being sent to Long Island to live with my sister." Dimly I recall her much older sister—a Susan look-alike, black-haired and beautiful, who wears turquoise-framed glasses. This sister, married and living in a private house, has volunteered to take Susan.

"My mother is giving me away," Susan says, without emotion. "She never liked me."

Within days Susan is driven away, in a Chevrolet. This time, intimidated by her mother, I run several feet behind the car, but do not call out her name. The last I see of Susan: the back of her head, the short black curls, as the car takes a sharp right and heads toward the bridge.

Only two months later, as the new school year starts, Mrs. Hassan remarries—a man down the block. She moves out of AnaMor Towers and into his building. On the day they move, I am playing ball out front when I see a familiar piece of furniture being dumped, by moving men, on the curb.

I recognize the small blond wood frame and narrow striped mattress. It's Susan's bed.

*D*iana is missing. The police have been called. The neighborhood is searched. Her mother sits, weeping, deeper than ever in her chair and resignation. The feeling is that Diana is dead. No child has ever *not come home*.

She has been gone overnight. "Overnight" is the key word, for Diana is always missing in the sense that she disappears for hours at a stretch. But never, ever overnight.

If she isn't dead, she must be kidnapped. No nine-year-old child has ever been gone overnight. When I hear Diana is missing, I tear through the neighborhood, hoping to find her in one of our many hideouts. I search the "fort" at the edge of the demolition site, the lot where we play on our oil-can platform shoes, the secret sewer pipe that we call "the cave" . . . and then, with a prickle up my spine, the dark park.

I never go into the dark park alone. Always I have gone with Diana or my uncles. Now, hunting for Diana, or some sign of her, I run inside, before my courage fails. It is autumn: the fallen leaves rustle underfoot, as I call, "Diana . . . Diana . . ."

I run down the footpath to the largest tree, which casts a circular shadow and in whose shade we sat out long summer afternoons. Our improvised chairs (made from wooden planks and rubble stone) are still there, so is our campfire, even my secret supply of seed pods (stored against winter emergencies that are anticipated). Heart hitting my rib cage, producing a visible beat against my tee-shirt, I tiptoe toward Pervert Rock.

Diana isn't there, but there's so much tension I know someone is. A twig snaps. The sound ricochets. I spin around.

Sure enough, a man, wearing a khaki coat held ajar, is moving in a sexual stagger through the trees. His hand becomes visible, making the brisk, familiar motions. He is not "our" pervert, however, but an older man, with a bulbous nose. He comes close enough so I see the purpling of his nose matches the purpling of his penis. His eyes are focused inward—he doesn't seem to see me—but I see his face, an alcoholic face, with entire vascular systems working above the surface.

With a silent intake, I bolt, run pell-mell for the nearest exit . . . which lands me near the synagogue. No, Diana wouldn't be there. Back to civilization, check the courthouse—I hang, for old times' sake, among the tunic-clad stone figures, ape their sidewise walk, turn the corner of the sculptured wall.

I imagine Diana around the bend, flattened next to her favorite warrior. I turn the corner: no Diana.

Next I check the delicatessens, the ice-cream parlor she loves. I watch a movie matinee crowd pour out of the Earl. No Diana. Then, on a last hunch, I start for the bridge to Manhattan. I'm thinking, "Maybe she went to see the heads. . . ."

Out of the corner of my eye (where I seem to see the most interesting events), I catch a flash of red on the long outdoor staircase that connects the Jerome Avenue El train to 161st Street. There, descending in a stately fashion, is an almost unrecognizable Diana.

She is wearing a red coat. An obviously brand-new red coat, and a tiny gray fur collar. Her blond hair is brushed, her lips look reddened. Her hand is tucked into the hand of a middle-aged man, who, as I watch, lets go of Diana's hand and spins back up toward the station.

I interrogate Diana: "Who is he? What happened? Where did you spend the night?" Diana will only smile and confide that he bought her the coat.

For what? What did Diana have to do?

She won't tell.

There is an instant outcry on the block when Diana walks toward her own house. Mrs. Duval, visible on the street for the first time in my memory, runs bulkily toward her little daughter. Her eyes are streaming.

Diana. Diana. I hug her. I was scared something had happened.

Whatever happened, Diana isn't going to tell. Her missing night is a gap that comes between us: we are never again close.

No one comes right out and says it, but somehow this is the end of Diana, the end of Diana the child, anyway. She is nine years old, and something, now, is so set that there is an unspoken consensus that it is "too late."

Even Diana seems to acknowledge this. I see her sitting on a stoop, dealing cards to older boys. She has a cigarette between her nine-year-old lips, and her shirt is open to semi-expose her absolutely flat chest. She looks at me, but without any hint of the past we've shared. She doesn't even nod. She just deals cards, smokes, and talks from the side of her mouth. She no longer wears her stolen crucifix, or the rosary she ripped off St. Theresa.

We never say goodbye. She still lives next door. But from then on Diana is missing.

*T*hree strikes and I'm out. My new teacher is the Night Witch. Mrs. Aventuro is El Beasto, a black-haired witch who is breathing fire over the fifth grade. Her mouth must be an oven of decay: she exhales searing gusts of rot.

She's on my case day one. Why is my dress so wrinkled? How about a better hair comb? Am I reading under my desk instead of paying attention?

Worse, she seizes me for public interrogation "in front of the whole class" (a phrase that sends dread through my intestines, makes me beg for a lavatory pass). "Oh, no, no . . . Please not in front of the class."

She goes straight for it: What happened to my mother? What about the father? Who is raising me? Are they my legal guardians, or am I a ward of the court?

I dunno, I dunno, I dunno . . . By now, I am familiar with the sensation that accompanies any serious interrogation. I'm being squeezed into an upright coffin a size too small. By three o'clock of the first day, I can hardly breathe.

Mrs. Aventuro instills fears more severe than any I had the nerve to imagine: "Am I in a home permanently, or will I be moved to foster care?"

I dunno, I dunno, I dunno.

"Well, I'll see." An afterthought: "Don't worry; it must be in your file."

I make a beeline from school straight to "Blanky" and my bed; the pink surface rises up, like a landing strip. I crash—

"Oh God, I-wish-I-were-dead." If the dog weren't there, offering animal empathy, I don't know what I would do. But Bonny is there, eyes leaking tears of concern.

Etka, sitting by the window, has no idea anything's wrong. She's doing one of her "I'm so brilliant, I'm so beautiful" monologues that I can tune in and out, like a radio program. She's like a.d.j. She just keeps going. At dusk, I tune in again; she's still talking about her legs—the shape of them, and how unusual they are in a woman who also does brainwork.

When my uncles come home, I tell them about Mrs. Aventuro. Len believes me, but says to "give it a chance. . . ." "There's no way anyone can take you out of this home," he says, sitting on the edge of my bed. "We are your legal guardians."

But what if someone did get a court order and I was to be taken out of this home?

"Never happen," Len assures me. "We would escape to Brazil."

In 5-2, the reign of terror continues: Mrs. Aventuro demands to know, in front of the entire class, *what I ate for breakfast.*

I have the sense to lie. I invent an all-American breakfast, something I've heard other people eat: "I ate bacon and eggs, toast and jelly, orange juice and milk with..." I pause to find the most normal cereal, something above reproach... "a bowl of Wheaties."

"Wheaties?" Her lip curls. She breathes her own sour digestive gusts—a palpable disgust. "Are you sure you didn't have tuna croquettes, popcorn, and baked beans?"

How does she know? Who has betrayed me? Does she fly on a broomstick past our window?

Confronted with such specifics, I knuckle under. "I may have had a little croquette, too."

Can paranoia be justified? Did Mrs. Hassan tell—as she threatened to—that we live in a "crazy house"?

No. It turns out Uncle Len has betrayed me. Not intentionally. "Oh, no, oh my God... it was just a questionnaire, sent to the parents: I answered in good faith. I had no idea... it would be used against you."

I am already humiliated to the point that I consider never returning to school. In the yard, I walk a gauntlet of tormentors, talking "tuna." No, it's too awful.

I stay home from school the next day, and the next, and the next.... I'm not sick, but there's hope that I can become sick. I take showers and stick my head out the window, hoping for a pneumonia-inducing breeze.

For the first time, my weak respiratory system fails me. I don't catch anything. I remain, restless in my good health, tossing

on my little bed. I feel better when the weekend arrives; it's a relief not to have to picture the other children still at their desks.
The pressure's off till Monday.

I malinger another week, then return to school with a forged
absentee note: "Lily had a stomach [sic]."

Mrs. Aventuro's suspicions are confirmed. "What was wrong
with you?"

I surprise myself by telling the truth: "I lay awake in bed all
night, with numbers running round my head."

In a last-ditch effort to win her to my cause, I confide how
tormenting these numbers had become, an endless multiplication
table, a malfunctioning adding machine. "I was too drained to
come to school."

Oh, ho, ho . . .

Mrs. Aventuro takes out my file and writes what looks like a
novella.

She grills me. "Who has legal custody of you?"

I don't know what she wants from me. . . . If I admit I don't
know who my father is, will she make me a monitor?

"Who is your father? Is he dead or alive?"

I dunno . . . I dunno.

*A*t home I demand more facts. I have never quizzed my uncles, although I've thought of it. Now it is essential that I know, if only to stop the Q & A at school.

Gabe answers immediately: "I know one thing. He wasn't Jewish."

That's not the point. I need more than that. Gabe comes up with the equivalent of "I dunno."

Uncle Len is harder to question. He cries if we mention my mother. I proceed with extreme care. Late at night, when he is sipping a whiskey and smoking a cigar, I try to broach the subject. Fearing his pain more than anyone else's anger, I have to count to ten before I say the word "father." Our exchange—a few sentences—is attenuated. We take half-hour pauses—emotional scuba divers, we need to come up for air between dives.

The word "father" seems to send gold specks through the darkness between us.

I never have said the word "father" to Len.

I can sense rather than see tears in his eyes.

By 3 a.m., I have all the information Len claims to know. He has actually seen Larry—"just for a minute" and "not full view."

"He was at a dance . . . it was very crowded. Rosie . . ." He breaks off. Fifteen minutes pass as we struggle for vocal control. "She pointed him out and said, 'That's him. That's Larry.' But he was leaving the ballroom. All I saw was a flash, blond hair, the side of his head. Then he was gone."

Half an hour later I cough and say, "Were they married?"

Some time later, Len clears his throat and says, "I dunno."

More bad news comes with my half-term report card. A long line of N's—Reading, Writing, Arithmetic: "Needs improvement." But the true blow is struck under Grooming. Next to Hair and Nails a giant, black-inked *U*.

Unsatisfactory.

I am failing. The description is scrawled in a tiny cramped hand: "Hair matted, uncombed, disheveled appearance. Soil under nails."

The next day Uncle Len is sighted in the school corridor. I don't see him myself, but I get first-person accounts: "Your uncle is going into the principal's office." He casts a long shadow down the halls of P.S. 35. I peak around the corner, and catch sight of him leaving: a giant, looming even larger than usual, in his black Chesterfield coat and dark gray homburg. His most serious costume.

Uh-oh. I must be in terrible trouble.

That night Len shows me the note: "Lily is an absentee."

It's true: I have missed thirty-seven full days and fifty-eight half-days (the times I didn't return after lunch).

An absentee. That's me.

That is exactly what I am . . . anywhere: *absentee.* Dazed by sunlight on the windowsill. Hours pass. . . . A form of daydreaming accompanied by a grooming gesture: working the plastic eyelids on my Ginny doll, time-traveling toward outer space . . .

Absentee: Everyone at school has appeared more often than I have. Linda Kravitz has waved her pink plastic doll arm on a daily basis, the miniature twins have appeared even with colds, Steven Hellman, with his missing privates, has waddled in, to sit eunuch-like, growing wider and wider, in his chair—but . . . every day: he was there.

And I wasn't.

"Something's going to be done about this." Mrs. Aventuro confiscates my notebook, finds it crammed with sketches of mermaids and other semi-nudes.

Uh-oh . . . Uh-oh . . .

*U*ncle Len comforts me with a story of an ancient king who said, "Give me words that can apply to any situation, something that will always help me, in good times or bad. Tell me something that is always true." And his wise man said, "This too shall pass."

This too shall pass.

Not the fifth grade. The millennium might pass, but fifth grade would last until infinity. I would always have to face Mrs. Aventuro, and be punished, told to face the wall, reprimanded for laughing, or secretly reading under the desk.

No. It would never end.

"This too shall pass," promises Uncle Len.

To help me through the rough year, Uncle Len gives me a surprise adventure. He has always taken mystery weekend trips,
which he refers to only as "secret missions."

He never discloses his destination, but provides "clues," in
the form of souvenirs, which he presents to me on his return. This
practice harks back to our prehousehold days, when I knew him
mainly through his manila envelopes—the tiny gift paper parasols
and jade necklaces. Now that he is actually living with me, he
adds perishables. One night he returns after a two-day absence
with a bag of mangoes, and refers to life on "the island." (Later, I
deduce it was probably Long Island, but at the time I follow his
lead and assume he means a place more like Tahiti or Samoa.)

Aside from the exotic fruits that regularly return with Uncle
Len, he also sports imported clothing: a loden coat, "hand-crafted
in Switzerland." In fact, all of Len's wardrobe can be traced to
foreign origins. His suits are custom-made, usually in Hong
Kong or London, and his shoes usually have South American or
Spanish hand-design labels. (Later I discover he has bought them
all through mail order—which explains his habit of making trac-
ings of his size 13 feet, and constant measurements of his head
[homburgs from a British hat maker]. At this time, however, I believe him when he says, narrowing his eyes in reference to a new
Chinese-made jacket: "Oh, I acquired it on a secret mission.")

Now, in the throes of my crisis, it is too much to think of
Uncle Len taking off for distant parts, even for a weekend, just to
buy new giant shoes. "Take me," I plead. "Take me."

I never really expect him to take me—after all, as adults are
forever saying: I "have school." So I beg and plead without true
hope of satisfaction, and am thrown when, on a Saturday night as

Gabe "winds up the Shabas" (a Gabe-styled religious extravaganza that features a three-foot-long braided candle, and the waving of a silver spice box—"The Shabas must be said farewell to as a bride!" Gabe cries. It strikes me, every Saturday night, that Gabe's religion always involves him in spices, candles, and waving objects. It's pleasant. I participate, with a paper napkin on my head—my costume for religious moments, but it's not the complete distraction I crave), Uncle Len slips me an envelope under the table, and holds his finger to his lips in a swear-me-to-silence gesture. I nod, then peek: *two* airline tickets. Before I can open the flap and read the destination, Uncle Len retrieves the tickets, and whispers: "We leave at dawn."

Before light Len tiptoes to my bedside, and intones, "Lily, Lily, the Board of Education is excusing you so that you can go on a secret mission." Semi-awake, I stagger through my dressing and follow Len's instruction to pack tropical clothes.

Where are we going?

Uncle Len is "not at liberty to say." I will be "briefed" upon arrival. When we get into a Checker cab, Len leans over and whispers in the driver's ear: "Idlewild."

Idlewild. Even the name.

En route to our "undisclosed location," Len hints that our trip will have "political implications." In a fever of delight, I beg him to reveal our destination. He holds firm, for "security reasons."

Woken from sleep, I seem still to dream. At Idlewild, we disembark, carry our luggage—two manila envelopes (mine conceals a one-piece bathing suit), and Len's locked attaché case. He taps the lock with his fingernail and indicates: "The documents."

The plane, a Constellation, is spinning propellers as we board. Inside, the passenger cabin is empty, most convenient for Len's purposes. He informs me that we have chartered this plane for our mission. As if in collusion with Len, the stewardess bumps us into first-class seats. "No coach for us," says Len, nodding in appreciation. Another flight attendant, a man dressed in a white suit, patrols the aisle. Len points out a "suspicious" bulge at his hip: "Concealed weapon."

While our destination remains "classified," Uncle Len informs me as we lift off, leaving Queens far below, that we are heading for a "troubled Latin American nation." This trip is a diplomatic mission, his instructions are from someone high up.

Lunch is served—my first luxury meal: Filet mignon and champagne. While I order my filet "gray, please," and drink more Pepsi-Cola than champagne, I savor the experience. As we soar southward, I enter the hazy cottoned world of flight, dipping in and out of dreams. "You fly like an old pro," Len compliments me, when I surface, drooling, from a brief descent into unconsciousness.

The trip is so brief and exotic that it has the quality of a hallucination. I don't know, until we begin our real descent, that we are headed for Cuba.

"Habana" airport: On the tarmac, Len and I are surrounded by ruffle-shirted mariachis, singing and saying "Welcome . . . bienvenida" to Uncle Len and me, who seem to be the only two Americans visiting. As we stride toward the terminal, Len reveals that with Castro newly in power, all normal tourism has concluded.

There are no other tourists registered at our hotel. The hotel, brand-new, is deserted except for a skeleton staff and Castro's soldiers, who stand, holding rifles and wearing bandoliers, packed with what I call "lipsticks" of ammunition, in the red-and-gold lobby. This lobby is even more gilded than the Concourse Plaza, my former standard of luxury accommodation.

The exterior of the hotel is a modern high-rise, more grandiose than AnaMor Towers, but otherwise not unlike other luxury apartment towers, except that this hotel is pitted with bullet holes, and still smeared with red, which I assume is dried blood, spelling out the message: "Muerte a Batista," "Death to Batista."

"Batista left," Len explains, as we cross the carpeted lobby to check in. "So we are dealing with Fidel Castro now." We register, then peek into the casino—deserted—and then an entertainment lounge where a lone showgirl in heavy plumage is rehearsing, in a wan way, as if without expectation that she will ever again go on, her version of "C'est Si Bon."

My main concern is the swimming pool. As on a trip to Cascades, I have brought my suit and will not be satisfied unless I swim. So, even before checking out our suite, Len whisks me to the rooftop, where a turquoise Olympic-size pool shimmers under the Cuban sun.

The pool, the cabañas, the chaises . . . all unoccupied. There are no other guests. Yet a lifeguard, tanned and smiling, sits sentry on a high platform chair. Behind him, a soldier aims his rifle at the water, as if a counter-revolutionary might yet surface.

I can't help but stare at the soldier. He has waist-long black hair. I have never seen a man with long hair before, except for Diana's Jesus in the red recess of her church. This man seems sex-crossed, with his long ringlets and full facial hair.

"The Barbudos," Len says. "The bearded ones."

Len tips his homburg at the lifeguard, and the Barbudo then nods, as if they should be aware of our presence. "You're doing an excellent job," he compliments them. "The pool seems secure."

They smile, without seeming to comprehend.

I change into my pink one-piece in a cabaña, emerge for a solitary dip. The three men—Len, the lifeguard, and the armed soldier—all watch, with serious expressions, as I do ten dog-paddle laps.

Downstairs, our suite appears worthy of what Len now claims is "a presidential mission." On a high floor, decorated in black marble, with golden draperies—two "capacious" (Len's word) rooms with connecting balconies and baths. Len performs a ritual—testing all the faucets. He raps his fist against the walls also. "The room is probably wired," he mouths.

Just as well, for unseen spies may also benefit from Len's philosophy, expressed as he leans back in an armchair to sip his room-service Scotch-and-water: "There are very few of life's problems that can't be alleviated by leaving the country and checking into a good hotel."

Later I sleep in fathoms-deep exhaustion, wake to the surprise of not being in 7G but in a high-rise black marble bedroom high above "Habana." We stay for one day. Early in the day Len excuses himself for a "secret mission." He implies he has an audience with a "certain personage," who may or may not be Fidel Castro himself. He takes his locked attaché case with him, adding that he hopes to get material for his Ph.D. thesis. His next academic goal is to get a doctorate in economics, and he feels the visit to El Presidente will help them both. Len has insights, he claims, into the effect of the revolution on the Cuban economy, and he hopes Castro may add some inside information, so that Len can complete his thesis back at NYU Uptown.

He is gone for only an hour, and never comments on the success of the mission. We attempt a sight-seeing walk of Havana, but are instantly accosted by boys and beggars. The beggars seem close to becoming muggers as they edge us to a crumbling Cuban seawall. Len and I climb the wall, walk single file along the curve of Havana Harbor. I spot the main attraction—a sand-colored fort in the distance. I want to go there, I want to go there. . . .

We head for Morro Castle, but are hounded by the boys, who scream "Americano Loo! Americano Loo!" Neither Len nor I know what "Loo" means, but we sense it doesn't bode well for us. I balance on the decaying balustrade, in the style perfected back in Joyce Kilmer Park, but Len says it would be prudent to return to the hotel. For the first time in my memory, Len moves along at a real lope, taking giant strides in a straight line back to the hotel.

At the hotel we head for the bar, now partly occupied by what appear to be local Cubans, drinking rum and watching TV. Fidel Castro himself appears on the screen, and speaks for four hours without seeming to pause for breath. The Cubans nurse their drinks, and only Len appears to listen.

We take one more brief excursion, walking uphill, for a view of the sea. At the top we sit on a bench and stare off to the horizon. Far out in the Caribbean Sea, a thunderstorm—seen in its entirety as a small knot of blackness, laminated by lightning—spends its energies. Len and I watch in appreciative silence. So this is Cuba.

Walking downhill, we have our single in-depth conversation

with a native. An elderly man, bent over a pushcart, spots Len and cries out to him in Yiddish. "How did he know I'm Jewish?" Len wonders aloud, but we proceed to speak to the grizzled little man for a half hour, using a combination of Yiddish, Spanish, and English. The gist is that he was a prosperous peddler until the revolution. Now, for political reasons, Castro won't let him hawk his wares on the street—although, out of habit, he still pushes a cart—an empty cart. He spits his bitterness into the gutter, and curses Fidel in Yiddish. Len wishes him better luck, and we walk away. I ask for a translation and Len reports that the old man has said that Castro's soldiers are *"putzes."*

Len is pleased by the meeting. "It's good to talk to a real inhabitant, who has actually lived through the revolution." Yes, we agree, if we hadn't had this conversation, our opinions would be based on hearsay.

On the way back to the hotel, we hear what I call "firecrackers." Len squints and concentrates, analyzing the sound: "No. I think that may be a little shooting going on. Revolutions," he confides, "don't stop on a dime. They tend to go on, in short after-spurts." We see a few people running in our direction, screaming in Spanish. There is a sense of soldiers in pursuit, although no one appears. There continues a distant rat-tat-tat.

"Now," says Len, as we duck back into the lobby, "doesn't this give you some perspective on Mrs. Aventuro?"

I must admit: it does.

Back in the fifth grade, no one believes where I've been. Fortunately, I had mailed postcards, which are delivered months later, ripped and smeared with red, as if the postcards themselves were mutilated in the revolution.

*F*orsythia blooms once more in the dark park. The trees wear chartreuse lace. Two years have passed since Gabe and I first ran the footpaths, ducked under the yellow-blooming branches. "The chase is on!"

Rosie is gone. Susan is gone. Diana is no longer the real Diana. But the chase is on. Bonny and I run, connected by her taut leash. It seems she leads me—deeper and deeper into the dark park. . . .

A squirrel, albeit a one-eyed damaged urban squirrel, hops forward, pokes his chest with one paw. In the hesitant way of city squirrels, he panhandles for a peanut: "Do you mean me? Do you have something to give me?"

I give him what I have: a Tootsie Roll. He runs off to bury the Tootsie Roll under the tree where Diana and I worshiped our gods. Here are the tree stumps and stones that we said contained spirits.

Even in a city park the earth smell rises. Birds sing. The squirrel chatters (busy, irritated: "What do I do with a Tootsie Roll?"). The air is sweet and grassy, with the scent of onion. A new brook runs, sparkling, between our "holy" stones, charting a virgin course downhill toward the place where the park drops off. . . .

Except for the sounds of nature, there is a sacred silence. The moment calls for communion: I kneel, catch the running water in my hands, and sip. . . .

It is a moment to savor, and remember—especially the next morning, when I wake up with a 104-degree fever. My new brook turns out to be spring runoff, all right—from a disconnected sewer. While the doctor runs tests, my uncles retrace my steps and find the source: contaminated water.

At home in my bed I lie "dying."

"Scarlet fever isn't as serious as it used to be," the doctor tells my uncles. "We can treat her with antibiotics. . . ."

"Not too many," Gabe cautions.

I turn scarlet; the rash is really a design (you can see that when you have it tattooed to your skin). Up close I look just like a comic-book redskin—composed of thousands of red dots.

The fever is not altogether unpleasant. Sometimes, I'm high as the sky. But my uncles lie sleepless on the floor beside my bed, charting my progress on an improvised medical chart. They pour fluids down my throat. Between sieges of scorching heat, there are intervals of chill, and I lie there, shivering so violently I feel I may levitate. At least I don't have to go to school.

Uncle Len is so distraught he wears a stethoscope to check his own heartbeat, to see if he's dying from the anxiety. Uncle Gabe keens in prayer, rushes back and forth to *shul* to send up special requests.

On my "deathbed," I convert from the gods of the dark park, from Aphrodite, Zeus, Hera, Osiris. I give myself over, finally, to the One God, the Greatest Spirit, and ask for his help in hanging around the apartment.

Uncle Len is weeping. He will get specialists; he will fly them in from Europe.

Etka from Minsk offers European remedies, recalled from her own childhood: "We used a sock, filled with hot salt, wrapped around the neck." Also long crystalline stalactites of rock candy. The sock-and-rock cure. The hot sock is duly tied around my throat, where it immediately turns my neck an even brighter red, and I sip the rock candy from glasses of lemonade, as it dissolves.

The other members of the family take turns sleeping on the floor beside my bed. Even though other beds and cots could be brought in, there is a sense that someone lying on floorboards can provide more serious support.

"I'm dying, I'm dying," I say, not adverse to upping the already high emotional ante.

Throughout the long, sleepless nights of the sickness, my uncles take turns reading aloud to me. They have discovered a surprising number of novels that tell tales of nieces being happily raised by uncles, and these stories are, far and away, our favorites.

The Secret Garden has a particularly tonic effect. Even in a delirium I enjoy the saga of the little Miss Mary orphaned in India, being sent to live with a mysterious uncle in an English countryside estate. I particularly enjoy Len's reading of the sequences in England. His pronunciation of "Misselthwaite Manor" alone lifts my spirit. As he intones, in false Yorkshire accents, how Miss Mary flourishes, tending the secret garden, then helps her small hunchback cousin Colin to discover he is not really a hunchback after all, I can't help but feel much better myself.

So we spend night after night in Misselthwaite Manor, until I feel well enough (but not eager) to return to school. I am weak but well. My red skin peels off in sheets. I feel if I rise too suddenly from my bed I may leave my old outer self, like a snakeskin, behind.

*A*s soon as possible, I suffer a series of "relapses" so I can return to the comfort of home. My uncles take sick days themselves so that they can tend to me. It's a thrill to be a semi-invalid in 7G. Treats are constantly being brought to me. Now that I am well enough to enjoy a convalescence, I embrace it as a lifestyle. I may be destined to be the Camille of the Bronx, forever listening for the *squish* of an orange in the juicer.

Len is especially solicitous, preparing full-course meals in his pressure cooker to tempt my appetite. He never disputes my claims that I am running a temperature; he agrees—it is best to take the day off, to stay "on the safe side."

My eventual return to school is only halfhearted—that is, I last half the day. When I come home for lunch, I usually stay there. I am aided and abetted by Etka, who feeds me quarters, like a meter, to "keep her company."

After the original thrill of not going to class, malaise sets in—truancy has its own punishment. I have a sensation of forever being in the wrong place, in bed, reading love comics, instead of at school, learning the multiplication tables. As the day passes, another body clock ticks—as a parallel existence proceeds three blocks away in P.S. 35. "They're having Science Hour now" is the sort of thought that pops into mind as I spoon hot-fudge sundaes with Etka.

There is always a feeling that this life of illicit luxury will end, and sure enough it does. By the time the summons from the outside arrives, I'm so feverish and satiated from hanging around the apartment that it's impossible to tell if I am sick or not. I have slept twelve hours a night, and I toss around by daylight, trying to dive back down to oblivion.

A letter arrives from the principal's office. The dread words are printed on the page, words I would have feared if I had had the imagination to invent them: "HOME VISIT."

Home visit. They, the forces of law and order, representatives of the dread Board of Ed are coming to AnaMor Towers, to 7G: "To review my situation."

I had feared many fates, but not this one: Mrs. Aventuro and the principal belonged in P.S. 35. It seemed impossible, like an invasion from Mars, that they could intrude on our dinette, and worse yet, The Girls' Room.

Teachers in my home. If I survive the visit, I can consider suicide when they leave (fifth grader found in an incinerator shaft). Why me? I wonder. I have known other girls—Diana—who disobeyed at school, and no one ever invaded their homes. Diana had never had a dental note. She was truant more often than I was, and all they did to her was put her in a special section with other disturbed kids, including a boy who killed cats.

Forever feeling guilty, I knew in my heart I must have done something to deserve this fate. And what would Mrs. Aventuro say, after a tour of 7G? I can only imagine, and recall Mrs. Hassan's pronouncements: "They should take her out of that home."

I remember also the ocher-colored Diana—dragged from her apartment building in broad daylight, clinging, according to witnesses, to the railing on the stoop. And Susan, Susan, being driven off, exiled to "the Island," sentenced by her own mother. Oh, yes, the worst might happen—I can be taken from my home.

Why me? I ask myself at night, as I lie, my blood racing—fear has at last made me alert. Why me? My insides contract: I know why. My sins. I suffer mental flashbacks. The night my mother and I moved to 3M: how could I have let her lie on the floor? I should have let her have the bed. And then, on another afternoon, Diana and I danced, wearing drapery, for over a half hour, while my mother pleaded with us, from the hall, to unlock the door. I had stolen Valentine cards from the five-and-ten, moved soda fountain customers' change on countertops. I collected for the Red Cross, and spent the money on ice-cream cones. And last and worst, on the final night of my mother's life, when Gabe held the phone to my ear and said, "Say goodbye to your mother," I had made a joke of it, and said, "Goodbye," only it was . . . forever.

I had seen *The Bad Seed,* and felt the smart of recognition. I am bad. Deserving doom, I move deeper into deceit. Maybe I can camouflage 7G, create a cover. Fool Mrs. Aventuro and the board into believing I'm a normal girl in a normal home.

Still in my "sickie" nightgown, I step out to the hallway, and approach 7G from a disapproving Board of Ed point of view. Right away, everything is askew.

Even the dog, beloved Bonny, looks out of kilter. She runs sideways, her rear end angling to the left. Suddenly she has dandruff. She's salacious, too: she tries to mount my foot and ride my toe with lascivious delight. Much as I love her, I consider giving Bonny away, at least temporarily, during the inspection.

She leaps to me, lapping my face. Maroon tears run down her dog cheeks. She's so concerned she doesn't seem to note the flea that runs across her face. She loves me, and I'm disloyal. Another sin.

Still, the dog is a minor problem compared to the décor. Mrs. Hassan has said, "They live like migrants," and there is a transient quality to the apartment. Most of our belongings are stored in THIS SIDE UP cartons, which we use in lieu of end tables. Uncle Len is still opposed to furniture, so the rooms are sparse but have never achieved the deliberately attractive barrenness of the Japanese, whom Len would like to emulate.

In fact, Len's new bed, "the aircraft carrier," now fills the foyer. The bed, a king size, seems even larger because Len has it propped up at a forty-five-degree angle, the rear legs mounted on empty gallon paint cans. The odd angle is part of his health plan: "It's better for big men to be elevated. They get more blood to the heart."

And Uncle Len is interested in getting more blood to his heart, which he claims is "twice the size of a normal heart." Beside his bed rests a stack of medical journals, which he peruses, searching for symptoms he might develop. He also has a small library of medical books near his bed slope. As he lies elevated, he often reads aloud his findings. The latest, that Abraham Lincoln may have had a genetic condition responsible for his extreme height, is a condition that Len Shaine may also have.

Not so coincidentally, a portrait of Abraham Lincoln (the last Republican Len liked) hangs near the bed. I try to view this tableau through Mrs. Aventuro's and the principal's eyes: This Is What They Will See.

If they get past Len's aircraft carrier, they will enter the living room, which is worse. The room bears no resemblance to the artist's rendering of the junior four, which featured wall-to-wall carpeting and a "conversational grouping" of armchairs, sofa, and coffee table.

When I look at the living room, even I long for a living-room set, perhaps French Provincial. I crave wall-to-wall carpeting if only to cover the whitened, warped floor, which has buckled under Uncle Gabe's frequent Cloroxing.

The only furnishings are the gold-lamé Castro convertible and two file cabinets. The couch has long ago snapped its sofa spine, and lies incompletely converted, a herniated mattress protruding. Unattractive but not hopeless: I stuff the mattress ticking and entrails back in. If someone sits firmly on the cushions throughout the visit, the sofa may pass inspection.

But why oh why didn't we buy armchairs? With armchairs I feel I would stand a chance. The principal and Mrs. Aventuro could each sit in an armchair. Now where can they sit? Will they perch together on the listing couch? Or lean against the file cabinets? Sit cross-legged on the abraded floorboards?

No, they will undoubtedly head for the only seats in the house: the dinette. I trot over to the dinette, and regret even my own decorations. Why did I do that paint-by-number portrait of Osiris and Isis? God *is* punishing me, for worshiping rival gods. Oh, Uncle Gabe was right—there is but one God—his. I should never have gone over to the other side.

Now, what about Gabe himself? Will Mrs. Aventuro surprise him in full religious regalia? Will he be doubled over in prayer, in the doorway, when she enters? And the principal, Miss Riordan: what will she think? They're not Jewish—they won't get it.

Should Gabe pass Board of Ed muster, there is still Etka from Minsk, in The Girls' Room. What will educators think of my aged kid sister? Will she do her routines? (When has she ever stopped?) Will she give them her usual greeting: "You are the lucky ones to know someone in *mein* family. You know how to pick"? Will she sing—her own praises, and then those Russian and Yiddish songs? What will she wear for the occasion? My blouse, my kiddie jewelry. Worst-case scenario, will she mistake my teacher and the principal for prostitutes who have come to hook her two sons?

It is all too possible. No wonder we have always limited our guest list to only the most tolerant visitors. In fact, we have only one really steady "customer"—the single regular visitor to 7G is my grandmother's real kid sister, my great-aunt Dora.

There could hardly be a person less critical of our household than Dora: she may be the most affectionate woman who ever lived. As sweet as her big sister is tart, Dora joins us most Sundays for supper, and she spends the first half hour in high *kvell*—extolling how wonderful everyone is. She is a pretty, tiny woman with a heart-shaped face, and she becomes almost inarticulate with endearments: *"Ouchinka, Touchinka . . . Oogala, Mamala."*

Dora is ten years younger than Etka, and the baby of their original family. She is the only person who brings out my grandmother's maternal side. When they were young girls in Russia, Dora had almost died of influenza, and Etka had fed her mouth-to-mouth "like birdies," predigesting morsels that little Dora was then too weak to chew.

They recount this story every Sunday, along with the saga of the family emigration. They have one hot dispute that they also reprise each week: Dora insists it was *her* future husband who pointed to the picture and said, "If I can't marry this beautiful girl, I will never marry at all," and that Etka swiped the story for herself. "It was me," Etka insists. "It was my picture, *mein* husband."

There are other rituals enacted on these visits. Dora always reads aloud from a small notebook (yet another writer in the family), which she dreams of publishing in *Reader's Digest*. Her work is entitled "Happiest Moments in My Life." The fact is that Dora's life has been more than usually tragic—her husband died at twenty-nine, in a fall from a factory window, leaving Dora, at twenty-four, with three babies to raise by herself. She had lived on a string and a prayer—supporting her family by sewing corsets. Yet, as she read aloud, she recounted only the highlights—how happy she was on her wedding day, how happy on the day her daughter was born. . . .

It always struck me as sadder than if Dora had recounted her losses, and we all usually brimmed with tears as she went from one "happy highlight" to the next. Dora was perhaps subliminally aware of the bittersweet nature of her recitations, because she always brought jars of her own candied orange peels along as a gift. The candied peels were too bitter to eat, so each week we stored the jar alongside the previous week's offering.

This was the extent of visiting at 7G. Everyone else we entertained on the outside. After Diana's and Susan's departures, I never again felt intimate enough to trust a new friend to see us at home. I met my friends on the street or played at their houses.

Len, of course, maintained heavy security on all his friendships, although he was known to have many men friends (more than one named Igor), who were invariably foreign, or engaged in bitter alimony cases. Gabe had his long-distance dates. He traveled within a fifty-mile radius to escort ladies. His other cronies—songwriters with names like Snappy Schwartz—he met on the outside. Most of Gabe's social life revolved around the *shul,* where he could meet his cronies in the synagogue recreation room—there to drink schnapps and nibble the inevitable squares of honey and sponge cake.

No, visitors were not a common event in 7G. In fact, I had already worked up elaborate alibis, so that my friends would not intrude. My dear dog, Bonny, who would lick a burglar, was described to my school friends as "ferocious." One little girl, Sandra, was so scared of Bonny the Biter that she wouldn't even step out of the elevator on our floor of AnaMor Towers.

Now the inner sanctum would be violated, our household exposed.

Previewing the home visit, I see the junior four as never before. What will Mrs. Aventuro and Miss Riordan think of us?

There are shirt-cardboard signs Scotch-taped to the walls— posters for Uncle Len's campaign for President. Last Saturday night's family game was political strategy. Len would be our candidate, running on the "worry" platform. Pictures of Len, wearing a Lincoln hat and crayoned beard, promise: "He'll WORRY for YOU!"

There are other signs of eccentricity. Len hangs thermometers everywhere, to record uncomfortable temperatures. My grandmother has pinned family photos into long vertical kite tails, which hang from almost every wall. She likes to see us strung together.

There are other oddities beyond explanation: Why does our dog have her own room (the junior bedroom) when I don't?

Why don't we have curtains? Why did Len take down the Venetian blinds? (Because we were too impatient to maintain them—dusting each slat, then bleaching the cords, in the AnaMor Towers Hausfrau tradition.)

The light glares in at us. We move around on display, as if in a diorama of primitive life in the Museum of Natural History. There's Len—in his pith helmet and naval uniform—cooking up a storm in his pressure cooker . . . which has been known to blow up, and splatter the kitchen with his special fricassee.

I have an instinct to duck under some furniture. If there were any furniture I could duck under. . . .

Doomed.

Still, I make desperate last-minute attempts to turn 7G into House Beautiful in time for the home visit. I take more Clorox and wipe at the fingerprints that surround every light switch. Why, I wonder as I wipe, were we clawing at these light switches? It looks as if coal miners were trying to escape.

"Don't do housework," Etka advises, as I clean. "Play piano."

We don't have a piano.

With two days to prepare, I spend hours cleaning, totally preoccupied with such matters as a ring around the bathtub. I go deep into rubber crevices in refrigerator doors. If Mrs. Aventuro checks the egg rack, I'm home free.

Then—the afternoon of the home visit—I make the ultimate personal sacrifice. They won't get me for grooming. They may find fault with the apartment, with my uncles, with my grandmother, but no one will be able to criticize my uncombed hair.

With a pocketful of change, I go to the only place I know— Uncle Gabe's barber. I take a seat, surrounded by men getting trims.

The barber hacks off the waist-long straggles of hair, the hair my uncles have always complimented: "Look—Lily's hair has chestnut highlights in the sun."

Now the hair lies like a small dead animal on the barbershop floor. My head feels light. My neck itches. The barber shaves my neck with a razor, and all I can feel is . . . stubble. I can't quite give up the idea of long hair; the barber seems to sense this and, without having to be asked, packs my severed swatches in a brown grocery bag.

Short-haired, I run home, carrying the little bag. I feel I've taken steps in the right direction. Up in 7G, seeing me, Uncle Gabe begins to cry: "Why? Why? I always liked your hair the way it was."

I reassure myself: this is better, it will correct my grade in Grooming. Then I look in the medicine-chest mirror and see . . .

A boy.

*B*y nightfall, not only am I unrecognizable but so is the apartment. In a last-ditch attempt at simulating wall-to-wall carpeting, I have sewn two pink bathmats together, and stretched them out over a bad spot on the floor.

Much as I feared the home visit, it surpasses my fears in impromptu horror. There must be a God of AnaMor Towers, after all, a vengeful voyeur God, who saw my every transgression. He looked at me loonily every night through our undraped windows, and This Is What I Get.

When the buzzer rings, I try not to scream, but the sound rings straight up my spine. I count to ten, choreograph my walk to the door.

I already have new worries on my mind. After coaching Gabe ("Please don't pray while they're here"), I have a fresh concern— Gabe is not home. And he had been well-rehearsed to open the door.

Len is home—I have asked him not to wear the pith helmet— thank God, the temperature is too cool, anyway. But I haven't had the nerve to request he not use his pet expressions for me. I just can't ask him not to call me "the little *wutzi*."

I have toyed with the idea of training my grandmother to answer to "Gramma" or to stand, as if baking, near the oven, but that, too, is something I dare not attempt. The best I can hope for is that she will sit humming by the window. I do take liberties with her: I swipe the hair bows, before she knows what hit her.

Why is she crying? The one quality for which she usually can be counted on is cheerfulness—and today, of all days, she's sobbing: "My college diploma fell out the window."

Omigod. This *is* a crisis.

Two little boys on the street below have picked up Etka's diploma and run off with it. Uncle Gabe has run after them to retrieve the diploma.

Miss Riordan and Mrs. Aventuro are outside the door. Uncle Len is making waffles and Swedish meatballs, as "a light bite. Something a little predinner."

My grandmother is crying, the dog is whining along with her. I control my own urge to sob, and open the door.

Mrs. Aventuro, the Night Witch, fills the foyer with her dark form. Right behind her, Miss Riordan enters.

Uncle Len wipes his hand on his apron: "Oh, how do you do? You're from the board?"

He stage-whispers to me, as the ladies walk past us into the dining area: "What a lovely refined woman: the old style."

Why isn't he frantic, as I am? Doesn't he realize what's at stake?

Miss Riordan is not the person I expect. She is rail-thin, with hair so white it appears pale pink, reflecting her scalp. She wears a pink sweater suit, which hangs on her as if on a hanger. She is that thin and straight.

"Let me serve you a light bite," Len offers. The ladies take their seats in the dinette, and he disappears into the kitchen. The buzzer rings. Len calls: "Who's there?"

Oh, no: I don't even have a chance to rush to the door. I hear his voice in my head at the exact second Uncle Gabe answers: "It is I, another suspect."

Maybe they didn't hear him. I consider not opening the door, but Len is already letting Uncle Gabe inside.

Gabe holds Etka's college diploma. He is red-faced from exertion, out of breath: "I chased those kids ten blocks. . . ." He hurries to Etka's side, presents the diploma, which immediately restores her spirits. "Who has the most dear, fine family? I do. . . ." She's warming up. Her own crisis resolved, she can turn to our guests and notice the spread of party snacks: wrapped miniature chocolate bars, bowls of tiny pretzels, two bottles of cream soda. She pronounces: "Make a party, everybody will come."

On her party manners now, she rattles off a series of *"mein ohn* quotations," and throws in a few from experts: "I believe what Plato said: 'No company is better than bad company.'"

I hold my breath. Will she ask: "Are you ham girls?"

No, Etka chooses to hold forth, in keeping with the occasion, on education. She recites her own poem:

> A college diploma beats a lifetime of toil
> For every boy and goil.

For self-protection, I try not to absorb too much of their group conversation, which is a stiff discussion of exotic subcultures. (I suppose walking into 7G has prompted the obvious topic: insulated worlds where the inhabitants have their own language, cuisine.) Len is holding forth on the Pennsylvania Dutch: "They eat corn for breakfast, too. The Pennsylvania Dutch eat five meals a day: they wake up at three a.m., to have a seven-course meal. . . ."

They move along from the Pennsylvania Dutch, the Amish, Mennonites, to the Spanish Jews, who no longer knew they were Jewish but practiced unexplained rites in secret cellars, behind trick-sliding doors. . . .

At last—is it really less than an hour later?—Mrs. Aventuro and Miss Riordan rise from their orange plastic-covered seats. The plastic squeals at the separation. . . . Moving toward the door, the ladies back into the purpose of the visit: "I've read the report on your niece," Miss Riordan tells my uncles. "Her character card says: 'Lily is a dreamer and a doodler.'"

"Oh, yes," Len agrees, beaming.

"She lives in a dreamworld," confirms Gabe.

Miss Riordan motions me out to the hall. "Walk us to the el-evator door, Lily. . . ."

Uh-oh. The private confrontation. Already technically "out-side the home." I march down the corridor, babbling in my ner-vousness. While we wait for the elevator, Miss Riordan asks, in what I interpret as feigned casualness: "Are you happy here, Lily? Do you get enough . . . affection?"

How can I tell her about my life here? How do you describe love that need not be spoken of? Can someone tell Miss Riordan how high feelings run here? That if someone returns home late, the rest of the family will burst into tears of relief: "You're alive, oh my God . . . we were *worried.*"

No. Excess love may be regarded as worse than no love.

I button my lip and nod: Yes.

As I nod, our door opens again: My grandmother calls down the hall, inviting the two ladies to "Come back. This wasn't a visit."

Then Etka from Minsk delivers her kicker. As Miss Riordan and Mrs. Aventuro enter the elevator, they must hear her final compliment: "You know how to pick."

Do they?

I wait all night for a phone call from the authorities, or possi-ble arrival of child-care police.

Days, weeks go by. As in life and not in drama, for a long time nothing happens. Then, as an apparent afterthought, a letter ar-rives from school: a recommendation from Mrs. Aventuro.

Uncle Len reads the letter aloud: "I hope Lily's quiet days are over, and next year she will be a short-haired ball of fire." She adds it will be nice to see "more regular attendance" at school.

The next afternoon, the last day of the school year, I receive my final report card, which reflects the improved prognosis: a straight line of S's.

Even in Hair and Nails, I am now—"*Satisfactory.*"

*T*hat night I breathe easier, and for the first time in a long time my "Good nouchy" has the old, familiar spirit. "Good nouchy . . . wake up grouchy."

I tuck in Etka, who is the soundest sleeper in the house. Everyone else goes to bed—officially—but in fact rises to wander about the apartment at odd intervals. This is a nocturnal household.

In his foyer "aircraft carrier," Uncle Len claims to lie awake all night. He never sleeps—he only rests. He keeps a small high-intensity light by his bed and reads, or watches a tiny black-and-white television set, always without the sound. "It's more interesting to guess what people are saying," he explains.

Uncle Gabe wakes up so early to get in a dawn prayer that he can hardly be expected to sleep through the night; he wakes several times, in anticipation, afraid he might miss the morning rite.

Sometimes we wander to the kitchen or the bathroom and

pass each other, like ghosts, in the dark hall. This is a time we sometimes exchange whispered confidences.

There are frequent sound effects anyway—the quick slap-slap of someone's slippers, the clack of Bonny's nails on the bare wood floor. Mysterious shufflings, and, sometimes, an unexplained moan or call to God.

But there always comes a time when the household is truly at peace . . . sometime before dawn, after the final yawn-moan. On this night, I alone am awake. I sense everyone else asleep, and it is their collective breathing that warms the night air. It is safe, once more, to dream.

I was drawn to the ancient Egyptian rites, the tales of ships sailing down underground rivers. Often at night I imagined our family on such a voyage—gliding through ceramic channels, toward some ultimate destination.

We had once been four disparate individuals. Now we were joined for the voyage. Wherever we would go, we would go together, until death—or life—separated us.

In the next years we moved together; our course was set. We

moved literally—to another apartment, no larger or more attractive but simply farther north, in a neighborhood that was described as "better."

"Life deals some fast balls," said Gabe, and our old neighborhood changed (as they said on the street) as if overnight. The shadow of the dark park extended its radius. Screams were heard not merely behind bushes but on the street. The "civilized" park seemed to go dark, too. No one sat out there at night anymore.

AnaMor Towers was under siege. Unseen villains struck while the AnaMorites slept. In the morning, the ceramic eyes of the maidens were plucked out; they'd been blinded in the night. The doors were dented, the lobby furnishings slashed. Paint, like blood, was splashed on the sidewalk. The writing was on the wall: the message was "Get Out."

The neighbors, most descended from nomadic tribes, picked up and moved again. When a bullet shattered our bathroom window, we stopped praising the cross-ventilation and headed north.

The new neighborhood was actually older; there were still many private houses, oases of greenery. Our new street was as leafy as some in small-town America, the real America, as I thought of it. But the new building was almost identical to AnaMor Towers: Spam-colored instead of off-white. And what appeared to be Grecian maidens walked the new lobby walls—bearing sheaves of wheat.

Our new apartment was yet another junior four, the floor plan so similar to 7G that sometimes, late at night, I imagined I was still in the old place. The order of rooms was slightly different—what had been the back bedroom was now the front, an effect that disoriented all of us on our nightly rambles, as if somehow our family had been turned around and were living backward.

We moved by night (my idea, so our new neighbors wouldn't see our worn furniture). Etka, Gabe, Len, the dog, and I piled into a Checker cab ("a large one," as Uncle Len requested) and rode up to Roxy's Mansion.

Gabe, Len, Etka, and I were excited by the move—only Bonny did not want to leave home. She planted her feet on the old street, and no amount of tugging could persuade her to enter the cab. At last, Uncle Len bundled her into his arms, and we set forth. . . .

The night stood out as one of the few times we ate out at a restaurant. As we were unprepared to cook, we went to a luncheonette in our new neighborhood, where we all ordered grilled-cheese sandwiches—and one for the dog. The word "restaurant" didn't really apply, and wasn't usually in the family vocabulary. Only Uncle Len seemed to have experience with restaurants "on the outside." In fact, he kept a scrapbook of matchbooks from eateries with foreign names: La Medusa, Le Coq Hardi, La Buena Mesa . . . Uncle Gabe hated even the idea of restaurants. It says something about him, and the world in which he traveled, that he took pity on people who had to eat regularly in restaurants. He could not imagine that anyone would *want* to eat in one; they must eat there because they have no family. And, indeed, the highest praise he could heap on any restaurant was: "I didn't get sick afterward."

Etka from Minsk said simply: "My house is the best restaurant."

There was something special to that first meal on the outside.

We were going places together. I enjoyed the congealed American cheese on grilled white bread. As we sat in the little vinyl booth, I had the sense, still new, that we were . . . inseparable.

The move brought other changes. I made new friends. Because the move coincided with my change of school—moving into junior high—it was also a move into adolescence, and there was a sense that I had, in a physical way, left my childhood behind.

My first new friend was more "sophisticated." Nina was the child of "progressive" parents, who had been married at the Ethical Culture Society, instead of in a Jewish ceremony. Her father was a painter, who could not support the family doing abstracts, and so ran a dry-cleaning store. He carried with him a chemical whiff of despair at this compromise. Her mother, who insisted on being called Trudy, not Mrs. Leffer, was a librarian, like my uncle Gabe. They lived in a Tudor complex, called Ivanhoe Gardens.

It was there, in the Leffers' airy five-room apartment (it seemed palatial), that the new games began. Nina had a more clinical approach than I was accustomed to. She concentrated on describing changes in her anatomy. Often our game, instead of the scenarios that I was accustomed to, consisted of taking elaborate measurements and performing near-surgical procedures (on Nina—I wouldn't let her look at me).

We would go into her parents' bedroom—with her mother's permission. Trudy's approval shocked me—she seemed to know what we were doing in there. "There's nothing to be ashamed of," she'd call through the closed door. "This is the time to explore."

Nina would lie on her bed, with a magnifying mirror propped between her knees, and describe changes and development in her anatomy. I sat in a bedside armchair and observed her self-examinations. One afternoon, she plucked at her privates and announced: "I form wax."

I missed Diana and Susan, who were more my style. But I didn't know anyone else in the new neighborhood, so I stayed with Nina for a while. She could be as fierce as Susan and Diana— if not as fanciful. She was a brown-eyed blonde, with a turned-up nose and a sharp tongue. She would snap quicker than my new parakeet (called Greenie Meanie for her tenacious nipping—you could lose a finger trying to give her some millet spray). Nina would say, "Shut up" or "That's stupid," phrases I wasn't used to hearing from friends. She had a cute little figure that was develop-ing off kilter: her right nipple had puffed up, in preparation, while the left lay dormant. "It's not unusual for developing breasts to be asymmetrical," Nina reported, as she worked the undeveloped nipple between her thumb and forefinger.

I never saw a girl fondle herself before, but Nina did not stop there. One afternoon, as an air conditioner breathed in her par-ents' dehumidified bedroom, Nina instructed me to lie beside her on the double bed. "Rotate your hand down below in concentric circles," she said (her mother being a librarian, Nina had an in-credible vocabulary for an eleven-year-old). "Do you feel a re-ceding warmth?"

I didn't. And soon I stopped visiting Nina altogether. She was simply too clinical for me: the wax and all that. She had a similar scientific approach to her other bodily functions, and she always wanted me to keep her company in the toilet, too. I would have to perch on the bathtub rim, and appear oblivious to the sounds and smells of Nina relieving herself.

I left her in a fight over homework—she wanted me to do some of hers—but in fact, the homework issue was a ruse; I was more put off by her secretions.

She did leave me with one more solid piece of information. "The Man," as she always expressed it, "The Man goes *in.*"

No smudging? Susan had been explicit; The Man, according to Susan, never went in.

Nina was emphatic. She had walked into her parents' bedroom while they were doing it, and had seen everything. Her mother's only response was to say: "I guess life will hold no more surprises."

Soon I found a neighborhood girl more to my liking. Marty was an Asiatic-style Jew (with a bit of the Mongol-horde story written in her high cheekbones and almost slit eyes). She had hair down, as the neighbors described it, "to her behind."

Marty's hair—black, slightly wavy, and, when wet, actually touching the back of her knees—was her most outstanding feature, and our get-togethers revolved around brushing it. We were endlessly occupied, like primates, with grooming one another. I often slept over in Marty's apartment, another junior four, overlooking the Major Deegan, and we would take turns brushing. Marty would sit for hours, while I crouched behind her, working the brush through her long, long hair. Then we would reverse positions on her bed, and she would brush mine. We talked about our hair quite a bit, and always noted the differences in texture. My hair was finer, and still "growing in." An awful lot of our hair seemed to fall out during these late-night sessions. While we brushed, or perhaps plucked at one another's eyebrows, we listened to appropriate music on Marty's portable radio: "In the jungle, the lion sleeps tonight."

Marty was even shyer than I was, so it was up to me to arrange our social schedule, which was, after all, what this hair brushing was leading up to. We would go to soda fountains and watch boys.

We were not yet up to talking to boys, which was regarded as a special skill.

I spent many nights in Marty's house, and I came to know her family. As always I was curious about more normal families. Her parents had married at midlife, and slept locked together in a serious partnership on their converted Castro in the living room. Marty's father, Mr. Tourin, held on to Marty's mother in a spoon position, gripping the plump, gray-haired Mrs. Tourin as if his life depended on it. As, he said, it did: "I only wish I had met her twenty years sooner."

Mrs. Tourin, who often came into Marty's room to chat during our hair-brushing sessions, said of her husband: "A man who wears a tie with a short-sleeved sport shirt can always be trusted."

Marty had two brothers, and so my visits to her house afforded my first closeup look at teenaged boys in their natural habitat. Her older brother, Mark, Tartar-eyed like Marty, was the only person I ever met who admired Howard Cosell. He wanted to be just like him. Her younger brother, Ira, had been born a month prematurely, and even now, at thirteen, seemed to be permanently trying to catch up. He tagged our steps, and sat, in a puppyish way, at the foot of Marty's bed sometimes.

My friendship with Marty lasted for a few years, and broke up when we started high school—an all-girls high school. I fell into bad company in the form of Sheila Kriszinski ("It's being changed to Kristin").

Everyone in Walton High said Sheila looked like Elizabeth

Taylor. In fact, she was only made up to look like Elizabeth Taylor: she painted heavy black Cleopatra eyeliner around her brown eyes, and wore her black hair in the Egyptian style. Her features were less defined than Elizabeth Taylor's, and it was apparent, even at fourteen, that she would soon look like her mother and Mrs. Khrushchev, who were identical in appearance.

Although her weight was still under control (encased in girdles, worn under her tight skirts), Sheila's body always threatened to expand into the wide Ukrainian shape that was her genetic heritage. "I can't wait till I'm married; then I can eat" was one of her oft-quoted remarks.

She was destined to be fat—not only because of her heredity (both parents were obese) but also because of the major environmental factor: her father was in the business of providing food, wholesale, to delicatessens. Their apartment—an old floor-through above a supermarket—was always overstocked with generic tubs of mustard and vats of macaroni salad. They had industrial-size sacks of potato chips, and ice cream in five-gallon containers.

The Kriszinski household was well-equipped to deal with these provisions. They had professional kitchen equipment. When I entered Sheila's home, the first sight to greet my eyes was her older brother, Carey, a massive three-hundred-pounder, standing in the aisle-kitchen slowly easing a roast through a slicer. Behind him, Mrs. Kriszinski, whom I never saw wear anything but a pink nightgown and a hairnet, was sitting on the lap of Mr. Kriszinski. They each weighed close to three hundred pounds, and they seemed to roll, on their bearings, as they sat spooning potato salad into each other's mouths.

I thought they appeared a loving couple, in a food-oriented

way, but Sheila muttered, as we squeezed past: "You can tell they don't do it anymore."

Sheila's family had some bizarre sleeping arrangements of their own. Sheila led me to the bed that she shared with her mother. "My father sleeps with my brother," she added. As the Kriszinski apartment was of the old railroad-flat style, one walked through each room to reach the next, so every bedroom was visible, as we made our way to our destination: the room Sheila shared with her mother.

She had three brothers. The big one, Carey, was forever working the meat slicer, and we inevitably would collide with him if we made our way to the refrigerator for a snack. "You're eating like you have eight rectums," was his standard greeting to his sister. I was shocked at his choice of language. No one in my home would ever say such a thing, even, or especially, if it was true.

The other two brothers were more appealing. Sheila had a twin brother, John, who looked remarkably like her. (People said he looked like Tony Curtis, but he came as close to that as Sheila did to resembling Elizabeth Taylor.) Sheila told me she could recall cuddling next to John in the womb, and they had shared a crib for several years. She still seemed to feel a tug toward him. She often wrapped her arms around his waist, hugging him from behind. She would sway, in a near-dance motion, behind him, anytime he stood within her reach. Until puberty, when John "had to wear a jock," as Sheila expressed it, the two had been inseparable. John and Sheila had slept in a triple embrace, with their mother on what was called the "big bed."

But, now that John was becoming more manly, he was banished to share a room with the third brother, Stuie, whom I fell in love with at first sight and who was my main reason for being in the Kriszinski apartment. Stuie was as fit as the rest of the family was fat. While the others spooned ice cream from the five-gallon vats, Stuie worked with weights in the center of the living room. He was different from them in every way, and privately I suspected there had been a birth mixup, and he did not truly belong among the Kriszinskis.

"Stuie, my love god," was how I described him in the journal I now kept, primarily to record a series of hopeless crushes on incredibly handsome neighborhood boys. I compared him to Apollo, who was my ideal. And, although I never spoke directly to him (I could not yet talk to boys), I mentally addressed him, and wrote sonnets in my diary, describing his "gold-fuzzed forearms."

I had dreams of bobbing with Stuie in a turquoise sea I took to be the Aegean. I never confessed my feelings, even to Sheila. I simply sat around the Kriszinski abode, catching glimpses of the love god.

Stuie worked as a lifeguard, during the summer, at Orchard (Horseshit) Beach. I had an actual plan, which involved a near-drowning, so that I might be resuscitated by him.

Meanwhile, Sheila expanded my knowledge of sexual matters. She had "sex texts" in her bedroom, and would read aloud, describing complicated positions for intercourse. Sheila herself was intent on getting married before she was twenty. She thought that after nineteen you had to admit you were old. She set serious goals for both of us: we had to be going steady by the time we were sixteen, engaged by eighteen, and married before that dread twentieth birthday.

She didn't seem as interested in the boy she would marry as

in the hardware he would provide: "First I want an ankle bracelet, then I want a signet ring, then the pin, then the diamond. . . ." For all her recitations of intercourse positions, she did not expect to enjoy sex. When she read the chapter regarding "penetration on the wedding night," Sheila snorted and said: "My husband will be lucky to penetrate the door."

Sex was something Sheila would grudgingly give when the time came—in exchange for freedom from work and the license to eat. For now, she kept her figure within reasonable limits, but said often, as she pushed away a vat of slaw, "I can't wait."

Through Sheila, I met the first girl in my real world (not in the confession magazines) who had "done it." Jan Foot lived in Sheila's building, in the basement. She was the super's daughter, and she seemed to come with the accommodation. Only fifteen, she kept a condom in her pocket—one that she reused, as needed.

Jan worked after school at the luncheonette counter at the five-and-dime, in a mist of hamburger vapor. She wore a checked uniform and a full apron, and kept the condom in her pocket— even, I noted, while she grilled burgers. She was having an affair with the five-and-dime manager, a silver-haired married man, who stalked the aisles, and whom, although she admitted to having all varieties of intercourse with him, she respectfully addressed only as "Mr. L."

Sheila wanted me to know Jan so that we could benefit from her experience. Like Toni Bloom of Camp Ava, Sheila felt it was important to appear experienced so that the boys would not dismiss us as "babies." "If you're not experienced," she advised me, as we sipped sodas at Jan's counter, "fake it. You can always bull it up."

Jan grinned—showing a permanent slime on her buck

teeth—and waved the condom at us. She did not have to "bull it up." "Don't go *that* far," Sheila warned. "You want boys to respect you."

She outlined the body boundaries: boys could touch so far and no farther. The mouth was the first frontier: grit your lips against penetration for the first date. "Frenching," as she called it, "would come later." You had to mete out small victories to the boys so that they would "keep coming back for more." On the second date, she suggested a partial tongue penetration could be permitted. On later dates, "he" could "feel you up" but not *under* your clothes. If I were to be so fortunate as to receive his heavy class ring—this lent a degree of respectability—he could be allowed to "feel on top" but "not on bottom." With additional fourteen-karat-gold commitments—ankle bracelets—he might be allowed to "grind," rub his groin against yours in what sounded like agonized ecstasy for time periods that could, according to Sheila, run up to eight hours at a stretch.

Sheila already had a bit of experience. At a bungalow colony in the mountains, she had briefly gone steady with a boy named Bobby, who she said now suffered from "blue balls." Blue balls were brought on by frustration, which could ultimately lead to a big wedding.

One night, Sheila became tipsy drinking her parents' cherry herring and sloe gin (the family spirits of choice), and admitted that she had touched Bobby's blue balls from the outside of his pants. "They were enormous," she reported, with satisfaction.

I commuted from the Kriszinskis' world, with all its wisdoms, to my family's apartment, where Uncle Gabe and Uncle Len now wrestled with teaching me the facts of life. Keeping my fund of information—blue balls, reusable condoms—to myself, I watched Uncle Gabe and Len struggle with the challenge. First they tossed the task to Etka, who, they reasoned, would give me a woman's point of view.

Etka began with a flourish—a tale that sounded like a Russian version of the Garden of Eden: "The boy and the girl walk into a flower garden. They exchange poems. He tells her how beautiful she is, and they stand closer together. He begs for a kiss. . . ." At this point Etka's good eye clouded, and she lost the train of thought: *"Vergessen."*

She had forgotten what comes next.

My uncles' next move recalled the days when they had phoned Great-aunt Dora to oversee my bath. They paid her taxi fare, and Dora arrived, in her usual bustle of endearments, with more jars of candied orange peel.

Dora had come prepared. She had brought with her a brassière, wrapped in scented tissue, that dated back to the Czarist regime but had never been worn. She had been saving this brassière—satin, embroidered in multicolored threads depicting tiny hummingbirds sipping from opened flowers. Dora made a small ceremony of the presentation. We went into The Girls' Room, alone. (Perhaps she knew if Etka saw that embroidered brassière she would try to swipe it for herself. She seized it later, anyway.)

"Soon you will want to wear this," Dora said, handing me the beautiful brassière. Then she twirled around the room, singing Russian songs of courtship. "Don't rush me, don't rush me," she trilled. "Don't rush me. . . ."

And that was the extent of my sexual orientation from Great-aunt Dora.

My uncles divined that the deed had not been done, so, late one night, as he sipped a glass of warm milk at our dinette set, Uncle Gabe mentioned that Talmudic law endorsed sexual love between husband and wife—in fact, it was *compulsory*. "Every Friday night," Gabe announced, with what sounded like anticipation. He then handed me a paperback text, *What Every Jewish Woman Should Know*, that detailed a series of ritual baths.

Uncle Len, always so knowledgeable, lost his perspective and became, for the first time, overwrought: He couldn't impart any information at all, but seemed on the verge of tears as he predicted: "Oh my God, boys will try to take advantage of you."

If only they would. Night after night, I entered the increasingly licentious land of my now erotically inclined Indian chief. White Eagle was no longer content to remain wounded, behind waterfalls and wigwams. Now he was what Sheila would call "horny." In my nightly scenarios, he rode in, his bone breast-plates a-rattle, his headdress a-quiver. White Eagle meant business. His capture of me became serious. Whereas once upon a time I had concocted elaborate scenes of woodland life, complete with props such as birch-bark baskets, now there was barely time to pick an obligatory berry. White Eagle would gallop in on his pinto pony and seize me as I waded in a stream. From there, he spirited me away to a secret clearing, where he pressed himself, mightily, against me. Who knew? Perhaps Sheila was right, and even White Eagle had blue balls. His loincloth became increasingly suspicious, and although I still loved him for years, I did not know where to draw the line.

My uncles finally slipped a copy of *Facts of Love and Life for Teenagers* under my pillow. From then on, my tortured dreams incorporated medical terms of reproduction. White Eagle began to complain of "congestion" and "engorgement." While he writhed on top of me, I worried increasingly that "fertilization" might take place.

Apart from my midnight imaginings, I lacked what Sheila called experience. She set new sexual deadlines for me: I had to be kissed before I turned sixteen, or, ominously, "it would be too late."

I began to pray—dramatically, on the floor of The Girls' Room—for a date. Picking up perhaps on the religious intensity, Uncle Gabe came to the rescue. He seemed an unlikely match-maker, as he went from one unrequited love in a distant borough to the next, but he did arrange the seemingly impossible. He fixed me up with a blind date.

"What's the rush?" wailed Uncle Len. "She's only fifteen." We asked him what he believed to be an appropriate age for a first date.

"Thirty-two," he answered, after giving it some thought. "In Ireland," he added, "most people begin to date in their thirties."

We weren't in Ireland, I pointed out to Len. We were in the Bronx, where dating frenzies began in junior high school. I had no doubt that my first date would change my life, throwing me headlong into romance and sensation. I was secretly interested in "soul kissing," which I imagined would directly touch the spirit, and inspire a cerebral and perhaps eternal connection.

I also knew, as Sheila stressed, that I needed experience. The kissing games I had played at camp and at junior high school par-ties did not count. The boys had been too young. I recalled games of Postman when the girls complained that, when locked in the closet with the Postman (he was to "deliver de letter de sooner de better"), the boy would beg off. The couple would observe a five-minute interval in the closet, to titillate the curiosity of those who waited outside, then leave the closet with a pact not to tell, which the girl would later break. "He didn't *do* anything" was a standard complaint.

But now the boys were rumored to have constant "hard-ons" (Susan's Sailor returns to port), and suffer from blue balls. To be alone with a boy now would be a different story. I had read confession magazines and medical journals, so I knew what to expect—molten passion that I would be *almost* unable to control.

No, the kissing games did not count—even when a boy pecked your lips, then fled back to his friends. The true ecstasy that I had read about could only be expected to occur during the emotional involvement of a real date.

Uncle Gabe had secured the boy for me, and swore he was unbelievably handsome. He was also Orthodox, a recruit from Uncle Gabe's Menorah Club. Gabe had made some recent changes, too: he had transferred from the private Jewish school library in the cellar of the Fifth Avenue town house to a public high school that featured vocational training. Most of the boys at Gabe's school dreamed of becoming mechanics, and Uncle Gabe had mixed feelings about being their librarian. A lover of literature, he was saddened to check out books on refrigerator repair, but he still hoped, as he expressed it, to "fan the flames." Many of the boys could not even read, so Gabe had his task cut out for him. Most often, his library was used as a holding pen for disciplinary problems. The boys would steal books, or deface them, but not read them.

It was a frustrating job for Uncle Gabe, made more so by the fact that he had to share this library with a beautiful but clinically insane woman, who on bad days believed the library was her own living room and refused to let anyone enter. She would lock the door and dust.

The saving grace was that Gabe was allowed to gather the tiny flock of Jewish vocational students—there were four of them—into the library during off hours and drill them in Judaic customs. He made them all wear yarmulkes. They sang Hebrew songs and celebrated all Jewish holidays. I believe the boys came for the kosher refreshments: Gabe served Manischewitz wine ("Man-oh-Man-oh-Man-Shevitz!" the boys sang). There was one black boy, an African Jew, who Gabe said was from the lost tribe, and who went by the unlikely name of Abdul Schwartz. Abdul and a boy named Robert Siddell were Gabe's favorites. They sang Hebrew songs nonstop, and enacted playlets in which they portrayed, respectively, the Pharaoh Ramses and the prophet Moses.

When Gabe told me the good news, I too became a believer. Robert Siddell, who was described as blond, blue-eyed, a young Paul Newman (it seemed no one could coast on their own merits; they must be compared to movie stars)—this young Hebraic hero was going to . . . call for me, and take me on an honest-to-God date.

In preparation, I bought a new wardrobe, and made endless decisions regarding my grooming. Should I wear my hair up or down? Lipstick or not? Heels or flats? Stockings or knee socks? For the longest time, I debated whether or not to wear a brassière. Then, deciding I should wear a brassière, which one? Aunt Dora's Czarist brassière or the new padded one I had bought on a secret mission to a lingerie shop? "You'll always be small," the saleslady told me, pushing the padded one. "You might as well get used to this now."

I bought a double-barreled B cup, which pointed aggressively forward on its own and adhered to my body with a complicated series of straps. I also wore a panty girdle, on Sheila's recommendation, to act more as a barrier than as a garment. All the girls now wore girdles, no matter how thin they were—they were a kind of armor against the permanently hardened penises we expected to encounter.

The girdles cut off circulation in our legs, and left deep grooves where the garters attached. This constriction was also considered a plus. If we, by chance, became overly aroused ourselves, we probably couldn't get out of the girdle fast enough to act on the errant impulse. Sheila had a girdle wardrobe: white, black, and pink, with differing degrees of confinement. She believed that if she did, by mistake, go too far, the girdle might also act as a contraceptive barrier.

Sperm, those whip-tailed little organisms that we read about in *Facts of Love and Life for Teenagers,* could travel at such high speed that it had long been feared they might propel themselves up our thighs. "You can get pregnant even if you're a virgin" was a fundamental belief, and determined much of our behavior. No sperm, no matter how devious or agile, could get past one of Sheila's girdles. "The black one is safe," she said.

She lent it to me for my first date. I wore it and the padded brassière, and in other ways tried to contain myself. I was making a serious effort to control my excitement. I downplayed Robert Siddell's potential appeal. "He's probably a clod," I said to Sheila.

"Clod" was her term of disdain. One wanted a boy who was tough or sharp, not one that was a clod or a shlep.

I didn't know whether to believe Gabe's description of Robert Siddell. After all, Gabe was not known for his powers of description. This was a man who still could not tell chicken from fish.

So I held my highest hopes in check, recalling my single phone conversation with Robert Siddell, during which he had stuttered, his voice tripping over the "d" in date. "Can we go out on a d-d-d-d-date?" Yes, he had a problem with the letter "d," but I was still willing secretly to consider him a possible eternal love. He already had the power to make me nervous. While he had stuttered, I had trembled, hanging on to the receiver and feeling sweat beads, big as tears, track down my sides. With a prepared script at the phone table, I was not exactly blasé.

Boys scared me. They would have to be dealt with, certainly spoken to. And I had not yet proven I could talk to boys.

I had had a recurring disaster—fortunately concealed—on my visits to the Kriszinski household. There, even with all the frank conversation taking place and everyone else's frequent visits to the bathroom, I had been too shy to say I had to "go." Rather than ask to use the bathroom (in front of Stuie! Impossible) I had quietly wet my skirt. More than once I had trudged home, chafing. My social and sexual life seemed destined to begin with a burning friction.

I was often so agitated by the actual presence of boyness that I would be struck mute. On the street corner, or at the soda fountain, I would stare helplessly ahead, the world swept suddenly bare of subjects. This difficulty in conversation impressed me so much that I wrote in my diary: "I am convinced that people go all the way because they can't think of anything to say."

I kept an index-card list of topics in my shoulder bag, just in case. Anxious? Of course I was anxious. If I had overprepared for the visit from Mrs. Aventuro and Miss Riordan, that renovation was nothing compared to the steps I took to ready the apartment for the arrival of my first date.

I painted the apartment: again, orange stripes. And, more ambitiously, I sewed four bigger bathmats into an area rug. I cleaned for days, and begged my uncles to buy a new couch so that Robert Siddell could sit on it.

Gabe, with dreams of entertaining his own dates, went out and bought a gray sofa, with only a few lamé threads (my taste had become more subdued), and—at last—two matching armchairs. I spent hours arranging this new set, picturing the social group that would occupy these brand-new seats.

I also moved out of The Girls' Room. I thought it looked too babyish to share a room with my grandmother. At least for date nights (and I now anticipated there would be others), I talked Gabe into trading with me. When I would return, still tingling, I imagined, from ecstasy, I could sleep, grown-up style, on the Castro convertible in our living room. That I sentenced Uncle Gabe to sleep in the little bed across from Etka opened up a chasm into which I dared not leap. Would he change her wet woollies in the dark of night? I had.

Already selfish with sexual motive, I seized the convertible sofa as *"mein."* I imagined somehow having "cocktails" with Robert Siddell, as we sat and ran through my list of topics, before getting down to the ecstasy section.

By the actual night our entire apartment was renovated. There was even a new nameplate on the door (my uncles' name and then my own). I now airily referred to my uncles as "my two guardians" because I thought that had a certain cachet.

I peeked at Robert Siddell through the view lens in the door. Even slightly distorted, I could see . . . he was cute. Gabe had not lied or misrepresented him. He was six feet tall, blue-eyed, and blond: a young Paul Newman. If one squinted a bit, one might actually think he was Paul Newman (during his *Silver Chalice* phase, when he ran around in a chiton).

In my all-girls high school, Robert Siddell would rank high. I wished Sheila, Marty, Nina, all of my friends could see him. In our world, peopled by movie-star look-alikes, a young Paul Newman would receive the most stellar rating. The neighborhood boys could be compared to other stars, but the descriptions were usually amended to bear some relationship to the reality: "Troy Donahue but short," "Tab Hunter but with brown hair," or, more obliquely, a "Jewish George Maharis." A Jewish George Maharis was a great catch but no one could top a young Paul Newman, except perhaps "Troy Donahue in a 1960 Impala."

In a daze, I moved through Gabe's introductions, the door, the lobby, the walk to the movie house. In a blur, I realized the first departure from my plan—Robert Siddell did not sit in the conversational grouping I had arranged solely for him. He said something about "getting to the movie on time." All right: that was minor. A minor change in plans.

We sat through two hours of *Inherit the Wind,* in a movie palace that featured floating ceilings and actual goldfish swimming in the lobby. "Fancy-shmancy," as they say. I kept hoping

Sheila would somehow spot me—on a date. We walked near her house, but the weather was wild. There was no one on the street save Robert Siddell and me.

The walk home was high drama: a seventy-five-mile-an-hour wind sprang up, but in my determination to keep the conversation going (I feared a one-minute pause like a death sentence), I babbled on without mention of wind or rain. Robert Siddell, too, seemed determined to ignore the hurricane. We walked twenty blocks, heads bowed, straining against the gale force winds, and spoke only of evolution, movies, and our life goals. I was going to be an actress; he was going to be a TV repairman. "Maybe someday I'll fix a set just when you're coming on a program," he mused. Throughout this conversation, which I thought was going well, my lips moved stiffly. I was wondering what my lips would have to do next. I pursed and pointed to that ultimate moment: would he try to kiss me goodnight?

At the door, without asking, Robert Siddell pressed his lips to mine. I tensed, waiting for the sparks, the molten ache, a total loss of control of my entire body. I felt only a cold pressure, Robert Siddell's teeth behind his lip. He ground toward me. With my back to the door knocker, I waited for more—the dart of a tongue, that implement of soul kissing.

Would he? He did. His tongue stabbed through my lips, heavy, cold, with the feel of grit. The tongue entered; then, just as abruptly, withdrew. There was a corresponding twitch "down below," an automatic shift that felt like a flesh equivalent to the motion of the arm on my record player: a mechanical return to its initial position.

"We'll save the rest for when we're married," Robert Siddell said and was gone.

I spun inside, into the dark living room, where I imagined the new Castro convertible lay opened and waiting. . . . Planning to hurl myself onto the mattress and cry, I sailed through space and came down on hardwood. I lay on the floor, the wind knocked out of me, and checked to see if any bones were broken or if I was paralyzed from the waist down. When I established that I was unharmed, I allowed my original reaction to register. As my eyes became accustomed to the dark—I could see the unconverted couch sitting, smug, against the wall—I tried to adjust to what I was. . . . *Frigid.*

Frigid. That could be the only explanation. I had been kissed and felt worse than nothing: a numbness. I accepted a second date with Robert Siddell. Maybe I would yet thaw out, but that was not my true motivation. I sensed I would not thaw out. The very existence of a boyfriend, the possibility that my friends might see me with him, was too delicious to abandon simply on the grounds of sexual dysfunction.

At school, your word was not enough—you were expected to provide proof that you had a boyfriend. Indeed, the proof— the evidence that we were attractive to boys—seemed more crucial than the boys themselves.

Class rings, bracelets, Photomaton shots of yourself as part of a kissing couple—these items were satisfying. As time passed and I saw more and more girls sport the evidence, I sensed that the hardware was what was really essential. I don't believe we truly needed or wanted the boys themselves—not yet.

The boys, as I heard more and more about Them, were demanding and frightening strangers. They panted, pawed, drooled, refused to take girls home unless they "put out." Sexual and financial bargains needed to be struck. Boys refused to spend money on girls who would not go at least partway. They could call a girl "a dog." More and more often now, we heard of boys forming gangs or secret fraternities, holding Pig Nights, when they graded the girls as they walked through the door: Grade A, Grade B . . .

We not only heard about these Pig Nights: Sheila went to them. She took me, one night, and showed me couples "making out," grinding, under bare red light bulbs, on mattresses laid out on the floor. At school, certain girls were rumored to be "in trouble." The scrap paper given to us during exams had lists of "discharges" on the other side. The reason was always the same: pregnancy.

Our all-girls school became a sexually attacked fortress: each morning, condoms hung speared to our gate.

No, boys were scary, or at least risky. It was the talisman—the class ring worn on a chain around one's neck, or the ankle bracelet looped around your leg, that was desired.

I needed a talisman, evidence. On the second date, I secretly ran Uncle Len's tape recorder behind the couch, as Robert Siddell repeated his proposal, and his hard, cold kiss. His tongue probed deeper this time, then rested on my own before retreating.

Again I felt nothing, but I did note he seemed still to have his erection. (I imagined it was left over from our first date. There was no evidence yet to dispute Susan's theory that male organs became permanently distended, although *Facts of Love and Life* made claims that the condition ultimately subsided.)

I didn't believe he really wanted to marry me—I suspected he thought the words would help his progress. His fingers moved at an excruciatingly slow rate—an inch an hour—toward my left breast. I wasn't going to let him touch. (Although the night before, in my dreams, I had performed sexual rites with White Eagle, who then traded me, for bearskins, to the Ojibway nation. There wasn't that much difference, these days and nights, between the Sioux and the newly formed Alpha Deltas.)

No wonder I felt I needed proof that Robert Siddell had mouthed these words of devotion. The kiss itself did not record, which was just as well.

Robert Siddell disappeared, and I rejoined my friends at our after-school gatherings in the luncheonette. There our conversation centered on "getting someone." Our fears festered years ahead of schedule. Sheila predicted we would be dateless for all the Big Ones—Sweet Sixteen, the Prom, every New Year's Eve.

"Why can't we find steadies?" Sheila wailed. "What's wrong with us?" Other girls we knew had ankle bracelets, signet rings, even tiny diamonds. Some of those girls were homely, fat, pitted with acne. "Why not us?" Sheila asked. Then, after crunching through sacks of potato chips, guzzling gallons of soda, we could come to only one conclusion: "We're too beautiful. We frighten boys away."

Most of our fears were fulfilled. We *were* dateless for the Big Ones. Yet, over the years, I somehow racked up what Sheila called "experience."

I became a promiscuous kisser. I kissed thirty-six boys, most of them in my doorway, a few in the incinerator room of the apartment building. There, with background sound effects of thundering garbage and belching flame, it was not hard to imagine where it would all lead—*hell.*

It was a kind of hell already. I kissed one boy in the incinerator room for over six hours, until his beard stubble grew in and scraped my cheeks. Afterward, I confronted myself in the medicine-chest mirror, and saw that my skin was hanging off my face in long horror-movie strips. He had seen me *this way*. I wept.

I kept a diary of my dates, mostly so that I could read the entries and see that I had a list of boys who had been interested. Ruthless in response to the boys' behavior, I catalogued them by kissing ability. A typical entry was "Larry G.: Gushy."

The diary was kept in an elaborate initial code, in the fear that my uncles might read it and be able to interpret "G.a.I. G.f. 3H." which translated into "Gary and I grinded for three hours."

The list was long, but gradually recorded a softening of attitude and improved experience: "Harry T.: Sweet, tender."

It wasn't lost on me that I usually dated boys who fit the description of my father, as entry after entry recorded: "Six feet tall, blond, blue-eyed." I dated Christian boys (when I could find them). And, when I couldn't, I located (with the magic of subconscious searching, water witching) blond Jewish boys named Larry.

I was never one to fight the obvious. If I was destined to look for a Larry, I would go out and look for him. I made only minor compromises—I loved a Larry who was not truly blond but almost a redhead. "Strawberry blond," I described him in my journal.

This search, I sensed, was silly, but that didn't stop me. The fact that the boys' names usually rhymed—I dated more than my share of Larrys, Harrys, Garys, and Barrys—lifted the obsession into absurdity, which helped.

Meanwhile, I convinced myself that Uncle Len had secret

files on my father in his locked file cabinet. Afraid to ask him a direct question, I took a hammer and broke the lock. For my trouble, I found a thousand postcards from my grandmother, when she lived alone in Florida, advising her children: "I.B. what Plato said—courage alone is Great."

I read all one thousand of her postcards—which, in Etka's style, were written on both sides. She wrote in purple calligraphy around the address portion, so that I had to turn the card, repeatedly, to read this borderline message. This head-swiveling style was a kind of reprise of the bobbing back and forth I had to do in person, to reach her good ear and catch her good eye at the same time.

All my trouble paid off with a tidbit or two: Etka denounced Larry in one postcard border, but referred to him only as "that gangster." Women of my grandmother's background used the word "gangster" more like "rascal," but still I pictured my father as a white-tied Pretty Boy Floyd.

The broken file cabinet was not the only sling and arrow I aimed at my uncles. In full teenaged revolt, I often smoked on the street, and stood sulkily nursing filtered cigarettes in the doorway of our building. But my style still owed much to my uncles, although I would only refer to them as "my guardians."

Like Len, I loved to wear disguises, and I was costumed, à la Garbo, in a white trenchcoat and large dark shades. I did not exactly blend in at school, among the good girls in kilts and knee socks, or even among the trampy ones like Sheila, who wore black slit skirts, black stockings, and talcum-powdered sneakers. I wore large silk scarves, to partially hide my face.

This mysterious image was somewhat muted by the fact that

I usually was accompanied by my cocker spaniel, Bonny, who did not realize a sea change had taken place. She tugged me to the park, as if during old times, and if I happened to pause for a sophisticated chat with a local boy (we discussed literature in the park), Bonny might destroy the mood completely by arching her back and doing her business. I would try to ignore the warm drafts of odor wafting my way, and continue to analyze my favorite author, a Japanese named Osamu Dazai. It says something for the new neighborhood that I managed to meet a boy named Larry who also was devoted to Dazai—and had a dog, too.

My Larry (as opposed to Rosie's Larry, the original model) was handsome, a sculptor, and attended an out-of-town college. My first good romance. He took me to the ocean, a cleaner sea than I had ever seen—Jones Beach, and, as I had once dreamed, we bobbed together in a turquoise sea.

My Larry eventually vanished, too—and why not? I was only a high-school girl although I often pretended I was already in college. I kept on with my series of dates, which threw my uncles into fits of worry.

I decided I was too old to be called for, so I started meeting my dates in the lobby. My uncles soon caught on and stormed the lobby, announcing: "We're here, too." We used the lobby from then on as an alternative room. But we all sensed the end was in sight. I was moving out in stages—first the lobby, then the real "outside."

At sixteen, I begged and pleaded to go to an out-of-town college. Len escorted me, both of us in trenchcoats, to a state college in a rural town, three hours away by train. There, on my first night of Freshman Orientation, I met an actual American Indian, a Mohawk boy named John Runninghorse, who looked (if I didn't study his teeth too closely) a lot like White Eagle.

"Tall, dark, and handsome" was my second favored type after the Larry mode. I was thrilled to walk across campus, under the stars, with a Mohawk freshman, who, amazingly, declared instant love for me.

John Runninghorse took me to a forested nook in a corner of the campus, a move I connected to his heritage. There he kissed me, as I reported in my diary, "without biting, not slobby, just right." I might have let him go further—an Indian, after all. I felt, finally, what Nina had called "the receding warmth," only it wasn't receding so fast. But John Runninghorse said he intended to remain a virgin until his wedding night—a remark that shocked me more than all the wild moves back home. "My wife may not know," he whispered, "but I will."

I didn't know how to deal with this, so I sort of drifted away. These upstate boys were different. I could not cope with anything less than a grope. But I felt my academic year had gotten off to a good start.

Back in my dormitory room, my new roommate, an Italian girl from Syracuse, snored, adenoidal, even in her sleep. I couldn't sleep with a stranger there, so I stared out the window and looked southward, in the direction of home.

I pictured my uncles and Etka, snug in their beds, calling out their "Good nouchy"s. Len and Gabe had not told Etka that I had gone off to college. Instead, they were counting on her short-term memory lapses, and had said simply that I had gone to the library.

For a few moments, I mentally transported myself and flew through the heavens, and back into our window in the Bronx.

Now that I had left, for a moment all I wanted in the world was to go back . . . to find everyone just as I had left them. I saw myself back in The Girls' Room in time to tuck in Etka: "*Ya tebya lyublyu. . . . Ya tebya tozhe lyublyu. . . .*" "I love you, I love you, too." And my uncles, they would be there, too, perhaps wandering the halls, wrapped toga-style in their sheets.

There was no place for me in the world where I could go that could be as safe and as comforting. . . . There are homes you run from, and homes you run to. . . . Mentally, I was racing there . . . wanting to hear my grandmother's half-knowing jest: "You look familiar."

AFTERWORD

Our household lasted for eight years, and I suppose in public we always appeared an odd lot. Within our apartment we enjoyed our rituals and repertoire of songs and jokes. The differences, I believe, proved the rule: we were a family. At times we must have seemed almost a parody of a normal family. We were not unaware of this difference. Uncle Gabe, especially, loved to speculate: "I wonder what goes on in a *normal* family?"

My grandmother, if she could hear him, would insist: "No family is better than *mein* family." Uncle Len and I would muse, *"Are* there any normal families?"

Much as I admire Tolstoy, I must question his opening line

"Happy families are all alike." Are *any* families alike? If any families are similar, I would stack the odds for the unhappy ones. Sadness is isolating, but it is also universally expressed in fits of screaming and/or sobbing. I imagine happy (or happi*er*) families (for Uncle Len always asked: "What's happy? That sounds sappy") are more distinct, because joy strikes me as the more creative approach. When I visit a family, I feel I enter a new culture, a separate country with its own language, skills, and style. The more creative this household, the happier I suspect are its inhabitants.

While our junior four rang with song and laughter, and became the stage for our amateur theatricals, it would be an unfair simplification to say that we had "a happy home." Our home was formed in the aftermath of tragedy. We knew we would not live forever, and if that helped us savor every second, our memory of the past also tied us to it. We chose to live with a degree of pain, to preserve memory. Even today, my uncles may look at me and see a resemblance to Rosie ("The ears: they're identical"). We still weep for a woman who died over thirty years ago. Perhaps an army of family counselors or therapists would not approve. We don't want to be entirely healed; our grief, now subdued and under control, keeps my mother within our family.

Memory defies reason. So much of what I recall should not, logically, have happened. The details seem surreal, overly erotic. But I am certain of my recollections—I was too determined to remember.

My childhood games, our family's nighttime revelations—all seem to have occurred in a dream. And when I think back to that time, as I do daily, I escape into that trance that memory shares with arousal. The same buzz in the blood, the reprieve, once more, from real time. That ecstatic condition the scientists call "alpha," and psychologists know as "flow." I still enjoy these transports of delight, the near-optical illusion as the outer world recedes and the inner world is allowed to take over: powerful, il-logical. The radiance of the daydream.

While memory is subjective, elusive, a tease, certain truths are inescapable. My grandmother always covered any black object with a white cloth, but still, at the age of eight-eight, she died.

She died at home, in her own bed, with her family at her side. If she had to die, she died the death we might all envy. During the last days of her life, she simply grew younger and younger—she spoke to us as an increasingly young girl. On one night she said, "I must study for my tutor. There is going to be an exam." The next night, she spoke only Russian, and on her last night she smiled and chanted snatches of a nursery rhyme. In a way, she died an infant's death: her breathing simply stopped as she lay in her geriatric crib. "Black, black, you never get back."

I still have her notebooks, *Philosophy for Women*, and within the purple-scribbled pages, another Etka lives: "I am lying under a palm tree, near the beach, and writing this. . . . I love so much to write what I learned from my life. . . ."

After her death, my uncles sat—immobilized—a second "shiver." I was grown up by then and shocked to find them still sitting very still, weeks after my grandmother's death. Now there was no one to care for, and so they sat, with their private thoughts of what the last decade had meant: a household formed, a house-hold ending . . .

Within a short time, my uncles started new lives: Uncle Gabe went off to Israel, and immediately married. He married the caterer at the first hotel he stayed in in the Promised Land. She cooks delicacies for a man whose palate cannot discern chicken from fish. "This is delicious," he says anyway. "What is it?"

Uncle Len retired to mysterious "other concerns." He still sees the same woman friend, secretly, even though no one would mind. He lives in a southern town with a Casablanca air, and occasionally travels to "undisclosed locations."

There are still missing pieces. The family history must forever remain incomplete. Had my mother lived, I feel she would have told me about my father. Because I was eight years old when she died, I was left with the version she chose to tell a child: the saga of the handsome hero, lost in a war.

Who was Larry? What really happened? When I asked my uncles for more information, they could not even verify the spelling of his last name: "We just don't know." Hadn't they asked Rosie? No, they said, they had not. They respected her privacy. If nothing else, we are a discreet family.

My mother was thirty-five years old when I was born. She made her own way, she made her own choice. It was only the time and tradition that forced her to create a fiction.

My question today is: Why did she create so elaborate a fiction? When I imagine Larry fighting a war, with a dog at his side, I have to laugh. Rosie, why did you include a boxer (not even a German shepherd) in this strange legend?

Growing up, I exchanged one fantasy for another: my father was alive somewhere. I could find him. I added to my mother's story, and created a dozen alternative endings:

I was always walking into my father's office (still the sun-bleached war office), and surprising him. Having seen too many B movies, I ran with what clues I had.

In my mind, the melodramas unfold: I arrive by train in a strange southern town, to kick up dust. Why do I wear all white and that slouch hat? To me "the South" meant *Gone With the Wind*, or *A Streetcar Named Desire*.

I proceed—from the dusty street—to his office, or, better yet, an antebellum porch, where my father and I can fling ourselves into delicate frenzies of regret.

What actually happened was not romantic or melodramatic—it was tedious. I wrote to the Hall of Records. My letter was returned, stamped "INSUFFICIENT INFORMATION." I wrote again: How many Larry Moores could have been stationed in Miami in 1946? Too many, I was told. I would need the missing man's consent before his file could be released. Later requests to every imaginable authority were also denied. My father's name was too common. I would have to give up.

I almost did. My efforts became erratic. I might not think of him for months, then I would see an out-of-state phone book and flip to his name. That was how I conducted my search—standing up, in fluorescent telephone "communications centers." Uncertain even of the spelling, I worked the combinations: Moore, Lawrence; More, Laurence; even Mawr, Laurenz. I studied the listings: Larry Moore of Flat Creek Road?

Mentally, I traveled to Flat Creek Road and there he was— Larry Moore, standing on his porch. He stares, brooding over a Bourbon and the muddied waters of Flat Creek. In this scenario, his wife walks onto the veranda holding an empty vase. "Why, who's that, Larry?" she asks.

"No one," he answers, his eyes meeting mine.

My only problem with this version is that I rebel at its maudlin nature. I don't like melodrama. It might be my life, but it's not my material.

I never had the nerve (or perhaps the need) to telephone any of the hundreds of Laurence/Larry/Lawrence Moore/More/Mawrs. The closest I came was to draft a letter to be copied, "Dear Laurence/Larry/Lawrence, Were you perhaps stationed in Miami in 1946?" I explained that this was not "an emotional matter" but simple curiosity on my part. There would be no unpleasant scenes. It was not a case of anguish, I wrote, then realized I had misspelled the word "anquish."

Squish.

I never finished the letter, never copied it, never mailed it. Still, the potential drama lurks never too distant at the back of my mind.

Hope is sneaky; it hides behind reason. As recently as three years ago I might pause at a communications center to flip under the M's, in the book marked "Alabama."

Then I stopped. Just quit. I don't want to do it anymore. I ask my uncle Len to "tell me the story of how he looked" one last time.

Uncle Len and I sit in the garden of his cottage in Florida, a tropical place, redolent of gardenias and citrus, a place not so far from where Len actually saw Larry. Uncle Len tells the tale, as best he can recall it:

"I had gone with Rosie to the ballroom of the old Grenada Hotel. It was very crowded inside. I can still see the dance floor, so packed with people they couldn't really dance—they just moved in place. And Rosie became very excited. She stood up on tiptoe and said, "There he is, there he is. . . . That's him." I looked across the crowd—and it seemed to me that she was pointing out a blond man, but he was facing the other way. I saw his hair; it was very fair . . . sort of sandy. He was nicely dressed, and seemed to be a good dancer. But, before I could get a closer look, he disappeared into the crowd—not *deliberately* leaving, just being caught up in that great crush of bodies on the dance floor—and then he was gone."

Even this "documented" glimpse of Larry is characteristically fleeting. I swear to myself never to ask Uncle Len to repeat this story. His dark eyes, so like my mother's, shine with unshed tears. His voice is softer even than usual, halting. "Oh," he added, "I do remember . . . one more . . . detail. He was wearing a sweater, a special kind of sweater that was in style then . . . and Rosie told me he liked that style."

Uncle Len takes an important pause—he's delivering the goods. The final fact gleaned about my father: "He wore cardigans."

Now, *that* . . . is my material. I say goodbye to fair-haired Larry in his cardigan, and swear not even to think of him, but to use the time and energy on someone else. These days, I limit my Larry thoughts to filling in the blanks on "biography" questionnaires. Where it says "Father's Name," I write "Laurence Moore" (most likely spelling) and, after "Father's Occupation," I scribble "Aviator." (Why lose the entire legend?)

His absence may have benefited me more than his presence. If my early life's a fiction, well then, fiction is my trade.

The truth, I feel, is something stronger. I was raised by two men who cared for me, and raised me, against convention. I'm their child, not his. And I owe my existence not to him but to my mother, who risked more than usual to give me life. It was my mother's love that made me. I am my mother's daughter. I am hers.

LAURA SHAINE CUNNINGHAM is a novelist, playwright, and journalist whose work has appeared in *The New Yorker, The Atlantic Monthly, The New York Times, Vogue, Harper's Bazaar,* and other publications. She is the author of the memoir *A Place in the Country* and the recipient of numerous awards and fellowships for her writing and theatrical work. Cunningham lives in New York.